ISBN 978-0-266-08497-6
PIBN 10947498

This book is a reproduction of an important historical work. Forgotten Books uses
state-of-the-art technology to digitally reconstruct the work, preserving the original format
whilst repairing imperfections present in the aged copy. In rare cases, an imperfection in
the original, such as a blemish or missing page, may be replicated in our edition. We do,
however, repair the vast majority of imperfections successfully; any imperfections that
remain are intentionally left to preserve the state of such historical works.

1 MONTH OF
FREE
READING

at

www.ForgottenBooks.com

By purchasing this book you are eligible for one month membership to ForgottenBooks.com, giving you unlimited access to our entire collection of over 1,000,000 titles via our web site and mobile apps.

To claim your free month visit:

www.forgottenbooks.com/free947498

English
Français
Deutsche
Italiano
Español
Português

www.forgottenbooks.com

Mythology Photography **Fiction**
Fishing Christianity **Art** Cooking
Essays Buddhism Freemasonry
Medicine **Biology** Music **Ancient
Egypt** Evolution Carpentry Physics
Dance Geology **Mathematics** Fitness
Shakespeare **Folklore** Yoga Marketing
Confidence Immortality Biographies
Poetry **Psychology** Witchcraft
Electronics Chemistry History **Law**
Accounting **Philosophy** Anthropology
Alchemy Drama Quantum Mechanics
Atheism Sexual Health **Ancient History**
Entrepreneurship Languages Sport
Paleontology Needlework Islam
Metaphysics Investment Archaeology
Parenting Statistics Criminology
Motivational

HISTORICAL INFORMATION AND JUDGMENT IN PUPILS OF ELEMENTARY SCHOOLS

BY

MARVIN J. VAN WAGENEN, Ph.D.

ASSISTANT PROFESSOR OF EDUCATIONAL PSYCHOLOGY
COLLEGE OF EDUCATION, UNIVERSITY OF MINNESOTA

TEACHERS COLLEGE, COLUMBIA UNIVERSITY
CONTRIBUTIONS TO EDUCATION, No. 101

PUBLISHED BY
Teachers College, Columbia University
NEW YORK CITY
1919

ACKNOWLEDGMENTS

It is a pleasure to the author to acknowledge the hearty coöperation of the principals of the eight public schools in New York City in which the tests were given: Albion S. Smallen, Stephen F. Bayne, Miss Olivia J. Hall, Charles B. Jameson, Herman S. Piatt, T. Adrian Curtis, Frank A. Schmidt, and Thomas C. Halligan, and that of Miss Ella C. McNaier, assistant principal in one of the schools. Not only was permission courteously granted to give the tests in the various classes but every assistance possible was rendered to make the giving of the tests a success. In so far as these tests may prove of value, not a small part of it is due to their coöperation together with that of the teachers in charge of the various classes tested. To Professor Henry Johnson, Professor J. Montgomery Gambrill, and Professor Henry A. Ruger, of Teachers College, and to Professor Robert S. Woodworth, of Columbia University, the writer wishes to express his appreciation for their many valuable suggestions and criticisms. To Professor Edward L. Thorndike, the author is under an obligation which only the men and women who have worked with him can fully appreciate. Without the encouragement and assistance of his wife, Mary Adele Van Wagenen, in the framing, giving, and scoring of the tests, the working up of the results and the preparation of the manuscript, the work could not have been carried out as successfully as it has been.

CONTENTS

GENERAL RESULTS

DERIVATION OF THE SCALES

KEYS

APPENDIX

INTRODUCTION

This monograph presents the results of a study of means or instruments for measuring historical knowledge and judgment, and of the application of these instruments to measure differences between grades, differences between ages, differences between the sexes; the interrelations between (a) amount of knowledge, (b) ability to draw inferences from historical data, and (c) ability to judge character and motives from facts about persons, especially about their public life.

SECTION I

THE SCALES

INFORMATION A, INFORMATION B, THOUGHT A, THOUGHT B, CHARACTER A, CHARACTER B, AND CHARACTER L

The final result of the first division of the inquiry consists of seven series of questions or tasks graded in difficulty, and keys whereby the achievement of a pupil in respect to any of the tasks may be evaluated. These graded series are educational scales of the type of the Binet-Simon Tests, the Thorndike Reading Scales, the Trabue Language Scales, the Woody Arithmetic Scales and the Hahn Geography Scale. With these scales a group is measured by the degree of difficulty to which it can respond with an assigned per cent of correct results (say 80 per cent). When the history scales have been increased by the addition of a sufficient number of alternative questions and tasks an individual may be measured accurately in this same manner. For the present an individual is more accurately measured by using the number of correct responses which he makes to the series. This number can, by proper treatment, be transmuted into a statement of the degree of difficulty to which the individual would probably respond with an assigned per cent of correctness.

The achievements selected for measurement are (1) those relating to the ability to grasp and retain facts of American history, (2) those relating to the ability to draw inferences from historical facts, and (3) those relating to the ability to recognize different traits of character revealed in historical situations. In each of these achievements there have been worked out two similar series of questions or problems, each of the two series containing problems of increasing difficulty for any one grade, and being at the same time of an approximately equal difficulty as a whole. These scales are shown in the Appendix. The number in italics before each task gives its position in the order of difficulty. The second number is its identification number, by which it will be designated throughout this monograph.

The Information Scales A and B are designed to measure the range of information from the standpoint of quantity and difficulty of comprehension. The questions used are such that, in the rating of the pupils, variations due to differences in the judgments of different scorers are reduced to a minimum.

In the Thought Scales A and B, certain facts are given from which the pupil is to draw an inference in answer to the question accompanying them. In the easier problems the difficulty lies mainly in seeing the point to the question, while in the more difficult problems the difficulty lies in the selection of appropriate generalized information. Owing to the great variety of ways in which a correct or partially correct answer may be expressed by the pupil, variations in the ratings of the pupils due to variations in the judgments of the scorers are not readily eliminated. Such variations have been reduced in a large degree, however, by assigning to a number of answers given by pupils to each problem a definite score, based on the judgment of from sixteen to twenty-two advanced students in American history.

In the Character Scales A and B, an attempt is made to measure the ability to perceive traits of character on the basis of the ability to select from a group of ten words the three words which best describe the character or action of the individual or group playing a leading part in each sketch. In these scales, three words which were rated by at least four out of five competent adults as being adequately descriptive and by not more than one out of the five as being not more than partially descriptive, were mixed in with seven other words which were rated by at least four out of five competent adults as being not at all descriptive and by not more than one as being even partially descriptive. In order to determine whether or not the Character Scales A and B measure the ability to pick out traits of character or are merely word discrimination tests, a supplementary scale, Character L, was worked out. In this scale motives instead of words are used for fourteen of the problems of Character Scale A, the motives being selected on the basis of the median judgment of twenty-eight advanced students of American history.

The chief desiderata in instruments for measuring achievement in American history are (1) that the tasks be symptoms of important abilities really desired by the school, (2) that the tasks be not too much disturbed by linguistic difficulties so that ability in history, not in reading or composition, may be chiefly measured, (3) that the measurement of a small group, such as a class of twenty-five or more, be made with sufficient precision, (4) that the tests be capable of extension to alternative forms so as to reduce the harm done by special preparation or coaching for the tests, and (5) that the administration and scoring of the tests be convenient.

The reader may judge for himself concerning the first and second of these points. Concerning the third the essential facts are as follows: The tests being given to groups under ordinary class-room conditions: Information Scale A correlates with Information Scale B (using pupils of the same sex and grade) to an extent of .71 ± .01. Thought Scale A correlates with Thought Scale B (using pupils of the same sex and grade) to an extent of .74 ± .01. Character Scale A correlates with Character Scale B (using pupils of the same sex and grade) to an extent of .83 ± .01. Character Scale L correlates with either Character Scale A or Character Scale B to an extent of .70 ± .02.

The mean square error of placing an individual by one test is then (by the formula $S = \sigma\sqrt{1-r^2}$) about .7 of the standard deviation of the children of his sex and grade in the case of the Information and Thought tests and about .6 of it in the case of the Character tests. For a group of twenty-five the mean square error would be $\dfrac{.7}{\sqrt{25}}$ S.D. and $\dfrac{.6}{\sqrt{25}}$ S.D. or .14 S.D. and .12 S.D. respectively.

The detailed data on which these estimates are based will be found in Appendix I.

A composite score formed from the three A tests correlates with a similar composite formed from the three B tests (using pupils of the same sex and grade) to an extent of .876 with a probable error well under .01. The three A or B scales when combined and used to measure a class of twenty-five thus give a mean square error of less than .1 the S.D. of a grade. For a group of 100 the mean square error will be under .05 S.D. or about 1/120th of the range for a grade.

As to extensibility,—the Information Scales may be increased by alternates until the whole content of American history is included, so that coaching would mean a good general course in history! The Thought and Character Scales may be extended indefinitely, under the limitations of industry and ingenuity in finding and framing tasks.

As to convenience of administration and scoring, these tests are at least notable improvements upon the ordinary form of examination. They may be given to groups of any size; 50 minutes is adequate to exhaust the abilities of all save a very, very few; most of the scoring can be done by the use of the keys printed in Section VII without the use of expert judgment and without any special preparation. With some special tuition and practice a person of very mediocre attainments in history and general wisdom can score all the questions with sufficient precision for such practical purposes as measuring the progress of a class, comparing two schools, or reporting the results of tests under different conditions.

In putting forth this series of tests the attempt to cover the whole field of mental activity involved in the study of American history has not been made. No scales, for instance, are included which are designed to measure the capacity of the student to grasp and comprehend the meaning and significance of historical situations or of the changing standards of judgment, to measure the ability of the pupil to judge of the degree of reliability or validity of historical material or historical evidence, or to measure his ability to distinguish between statements of fact and statements of opinion. The attempt is here made to measure only those phases of the work in American history which are at present emphasized in the public elementary schools.

The difficulty of each question, defined and measured in a way to be fully described later, is as shown in the following table. In this table, I is the difference in difficulty between an information task which 50 per cent of the 4th grade children do correctly and a task which possesses zero or just not any difficulty. T is the difference in difficulty between a task for historical thought or judgment which 50 per cent of the 4th grade children do correctly and a task of zero difficulty. C is the corresponding difference in the case of judgments of character, motive and the like. The amounts of I, T and C are, at present, unknown. The somewhat elaborate course of experimentation and statistical treatment which results in these measures is given in Section IV.

TABLE 1

DIFFICULTY OF EACH TASK

Information A		Information B		Thought A		Thought B	
1. I*	−0.4	1. I	−1.0	1. T†	+2.0	1. T	+0.4
2. I	+0.1	2. I	−0.3	2. T	+1.4	2a. T	+1.5
3. I	+1.4	3. I	+2.1	3. T	+2.6	2b. T	+2.3
4. I	+1.6	4. I	+1.5	4. T	+3.1	3a. T	+4.6
5. I	+2.1	5. I	+2.0	5a. T	+4.2	3b. T	+4.0
6. I	+2.8	6. I	+2.6	5b. T	+3.5	3c. T	+4.1
7. I	+1.8	7. I	+2.8	5c. T	+3.0	4. T	+3.4
8. I	+3.3	8. I	+2.8	6. T	+4.3	5. T	+3.8
9. I	+3.1	10. I	+2.8	7. T	+3.9	6. T	+3.7
10. I	+3.7	11. I	+2.8	8. T	+4.5	7a. T	+4.3
11. I	+4.1	12. I	+4.3	10a. T	+6.7	7b. T	+3.3
12. I	+3.6	13. I	+4.2	10b. T	+3.9	8. T	+4.3
13. I	+4.1	14. I	+4.5	10c. T	+4.7	9. T	+4.0
14. I	+4.2	15. I	+3.0	11a. T	+4.0	10. T	+4.6
15. I	+4.8	16. I	+4.2	11b. T	+5.0	11. T	+5.3
16. I	+3.4	17. I	+5.0	12. T	+3.5	12a. T	+4.6
17. I	+4.1	18. I	+4.7	13. T	+4.3	12b. T	+5.1
18. I	+5.6	19. I	+4.9	14. T	+4.4	13a. T	+3.7
19. I	+4.8	20. I	+5.5	15a. T	+5.3	13b. T	+4.9
20. I	+6.6	21. I	+5.7	15b. T	+6.2	14a. T	+7.1
21. I	+5.8	22. I	+4.8	16a. T	+4.1	14b. T	+4.6
22. I	+5.7	23. I	+7.2	16b. T	+5.2	15. T	+4.3
23. I	+6.3	24. I	+6.0	17. T	+5.9	16. T	+6.0
24. I	+7.8	25. I	+4.7	18. T	+5.3	17. T	+5.3
25. I	+5.9	26. I	+5.8	19. T	+4.8	18. T	+6.1
26. I	+6.2	27. I	+5.8	20a. T	+5.7	19. T	+6.2
27. I	+7.6	28. I	+5.5	20b. T	+6.0	20a. T	+4.6
28. I	+5.4	29. I	+5.9	21. T	+5.0	20b. T	+7.0
29. I	+6.8	30. I	+7.0	22. T	+6.1	21. T	+6.7
30. I	+6.5	33. I	+8.6			22. T	+7.7
33. I	+8.1	34. I	+6.9				
34. I	+9.9						

* I is the difference in difficulty between an information task which 50 per cent of the 4th grade children do correctly and a task which possesses zero or just not any difficulty.

† T is the difference in difficulty between a task for historical thought or judgment which 50 per cent of the 4th grade children do correctly and a task of zero difficulty.

TABLE 1—*Continued*

DIFFICULTY OF EACH TASK

Character A			Character B			Character L		
1.	C*	+1.8	1.	C	+1.3	1.	C	+1.7
2.	C	+_.8	2a.	C	+3._	2.	C	+1.6
3.	C	+.4	2b.	C	+_.	3a.	C	+2.9
4.	C	+.2	3.	C	+.	3b.	C	+2.8
5.	C	+.1	4.	C	+.	4.	C	+3.0
6a.	C	+.9	5a.	C	+.	5.	C	+2.9
6b.	C	+.8	5b.	C	+.	6.	C	+2.7
7a.	C	+.0	6.	C	+.	7a.	C	+2.8
7b.	C	+.3	7.	C	+.	7b.	C	+4.0
8.	C	+.0	8a.	C	+.	8a.	C	+3.2
9.	C	+.8	8b.	C	+.	8b.	C	+4.0
10.	C	+.2	8c.	C	+.	9a.	C	+3.7
11.	C	+.0	9.	C	+.	9b.	C	+3.8
2.	C	+.2	10.	C	+.	10.	C	+3.6
3a.	C	+.8	11.	C	+.			
3b.	C	+.5	2.	C	+.			
4.	C	+.5	3a.	C	+.			
5a.	C	+.5	3b.	C	+.			
5b.	C	+.6	4.	C	+.			

* C is the corresponding difference in the case of judgments of character, motive and the like.

SECTION II

INDIVIDUAL, GRADE, AGE, AND SEX DIFFERENCES

As in the other studies of school achievements, so in history wide differences in ability are found among pupils of the same grade. The facts for the two tests of information combined are given below. The maximum possible score was 63. The range was from 0 to 25 in Grade 4; from 4 to 35 in Grade 5; from 5 to 46 in Grade 6; from 6 to 48 in Grade 7; and from 10 to 51 in Grade 8.

TABLE 2

INFORMATION SCALES A AND B COMBINED

	Grade 4	Grade 5	Grade 6	Grade 7	Grade 8
Range...............	0–25	4–35	5–46	6–48	10–51
Medians..............	9.0	16.6	23.6	26.3	32.2
25%.................	6.8	12.9	18.0	19.5	27.3
75%.................	11.7	20.9	28.5	32.6	37.8

The facts for the two tests of inference and judgment, Thought A and Thought B, are as follows, the possible maximum being 59:

TABLE 3

THOUGHT SCALES A AND B COMBINED

	Grade 4	Grade 5	Grade 6	Grade 7	Grade 8
Range...............	0–24	0–35	2–45	3–49	3–56
Medians..............	4.2	9.9	20.7	28.0	36.2
25%.................	2.5	6.5	14.6	20.5	28.7
75%.................	6.2	15.3	28.9	35.0	42.0

The facts for the tests of judgment of character, Character A and Character B combined, are as follows, the possible maximum being 38:

TABLE 4

CHARACTER SCALES A AND B COMBINED

	Grade 4	Grade 5	Grade 6	Grade 7	Grade 8
Range...............	0–23	0–30	0–36	4–36	4–36
Medians..............	3.6	8.1	13.1	18.7	22.1
25%.................	2.1	4.9	8.7	12.7	17.2
75%.................	5.9	12.3	18.9	24.4	28.1

The facts for the test Character L are as follows, the possible maximum being 14:

TABLE 5

CHARACTER SCALE L

	Grade 4	Grade 5	Grade 6	Grade 7	Grade 8
Range.....................	0–7	0–12	0–14	0–12	0–13
Medians...................	1.2	2.4	4.4	5.7	7.7
25%......................	0.6	1.3	2.5	3.3	4.9
75%......................	2.1	4.2	6.6	8.4	9.9

The differences between successive grades appear in the medians given above. They are:

	5–4	6–5	7–6	8–7
Grades............................	5–4	6–5	7–6	8–7
Information......................	7.6	7.0	2.7	5.9
Thought..........................	5.7	10.8	7.3	8.2
Character A+B....................	4.5	5.0	5.6	3.4
Character L......................	1.2	2.0	1.3	2.0

The differences between the grade medians being small in comparison with the range within a grade, there must obviously be much "overlapping." There is an amount that will be astonishing to anyone who has thought of historical information and power as chiefly produced by school study. There are many children in Grade 4, who have hardly studied history in school at all, who do better even in the information tests than some children in Grade 8. The facts are given fully in Section IV. As samples we may take the percentage of each grade who reach the median of the grade above:

Per cent for Grade 4
- 5.8 in Information A and B
- 7.0 in Thought A and B
- 14.7 in Character A and B

Per cent for Grade 5
- 14.4 in Information A and B
- 10.6 in Thought A and B
- 20.9 in Character A and B

Per cent for Grade 6
- 36.0 in Information A and B
- 29.2 in Thought A and B
- 25.8 in Character A and B

Per cent for Grade 7
- 26.8 in Information A and B
- 22.5 in Thought A and B
- 34.9 in Character A and B

These per cents would be somewhat lower for a combination of the three historical abilities, but it is safe to say that a regrading of history classes on the basis of the absolute ability of pupils to do the class work would, in Grades 6, 7, and 8, put nearly or quite half of the pupils in a different grade from that in which they were found. Much the same has been found true in the case of language, reading, spelling, and arithmetic.

TABLE 6
MEDIANS FOR EACH AGE IN EACH GRADE
INFORMATION A

	8½	9½	10½	11½	12½	13½	14½	15½
Grade 4.....	5.5 (83)	5.0 (193)	4.7 (126)	4.2 (62)	3.3 (21)	2.8 (9)	2 (1)	..
Grade 5.....	12 (2)	10.3 (46)	8.9 (166)	9.1 (106)	8.6 (49)	9.0 (36)	6.5 (13)	7.6 (7)
Grade 6.....	19 (1)	13 (8)	12.3 (91)	12.6 (181)	11.5 (115)	11.6 (74)	10.4 (44)	10.5 (10)
Grade 7.....	..	..	17 (10)	14.4 (69)	13.3 (146)	11.9 (104)	10.7 (63)	9.8 (27)
Grade 8.....	..	..	17 (2)	19 (12)	16.8 (71)	15.6 (165)	15.9 (130)	13.9 (61)

TABLE 7
MEDIANS FOR EACH AGE IN EACH GRADE
INFORMATION B

	8½	9½	10½	11½	12½	13½	14½	15½
Grade 4.....	5.8 (83)	4.8 (197)	4.6 (127)	3.9 (60)	3.4 (17)	4.5 (9)	3 (2)	..
Grade 5.....	12 (2)	10.0 (46)	8.3 (169)	8.2 (104)	8.6 (49)	7.3 (36)	7 (14)	4.5 (7)
Grade 6.....	21 (1)	12.5 (7)	12.3 (89)	12.5 (184)	11.6 (114)	11.4 (74)	8.2 (40)	7 (10)
Grade 7.....	..	..	19.3 (10)	15.7 (69)	14.0 (144)	13.3 (100)	12.3 (57)	10 (26)
Grade 8.....	..	..	18 (2)	21 (12)	18.7 (69)	16.6 (164)	16.8 (130)	14.9 (61)

TABLE 8
MEDIANS FOR EACH AGE IN EACH GRADE
THOUGHT A

	8½	9½	10½	11½	12½	13½	14½	15½
Grade 4.....	3.2 (52)	2.5 (197)	2.2 (113)	2.5 (52)	1.8 (25)	2.2 (11)	0 (1)	1 (1)
Grade 5.....	12.5 (2)	6.5 (34)	5.8 (134)	5.5 (98)	5.5 (58)	3.0 (44)	3.3 (15)	3.5 (8)
Grade 6.....	..	..	13.0 (59)	11.4 (139)	9.9 (99)	9.2 (64)	9.4 (40)	6.5 (13)
Grade 7.....	..	..	18.7 (8)	17.3 (44)	14.8 (108)	12.3 (102)	11.9 (65)	11.3 (27)
Grade 8.....	..	..	20 (1)	20.5 (5)	19.5 (48)	18.0 (150)	18.3 (122)	15.4 (55)

TABLE 9
MEDIANS FOR EACH AGE IN EACH GRADE
THOUGHT B

	8½	9½	10½	11½	12½	13½	14½	15½
Grade 4.....	2.0 (52)	2.0 (196)	1.8 (111)	2.1 (59)	1.7 (24)	2.3 (11)	3.5 (3)	4 (1)
Grade 5.....	12.5 (2)	6.0 (34)	5.7 (133)	6.0 (97)	6.4 (58)	4.0 (43)	3 (14)	3.3 (8)
Grade 6.....	..	..	13.5 (60)	11.4 (139)	10.3 (98)	8.6 (60)	9.5 (37)	9 (12)
Grade 7.....	..	..	17 (8)	16.0 (44)	15.5 (109)	13.9 (100)	10.9 (63)	10.2 (27)
Grade 8.....	..	..	..	20.5 (5)	20.4 (49)	19.3 (147)	18.4 (122)	16.0 (54)

TABLE 10
MEDIANS FOR EACH AGE IN EACH GRADE
CHARACTER A

	8½	9½	10½	11½	12½	13½	14½	15½
Grade 4.....	2.4 (29)	2.5 (171)	1.9 (117)	1.3 (44)	1.6 (24)	1.3 (7)	1.3 (3)	..
Grade 5.....	9.5 (2)	6.5 (25)	4.6 (102)	4.0 (96)	3.6 (43)	3.8 (35)	3.1 (13)	3.0 (8)
Grade 6.....	..	15.5 (4)	8.2 (55)	8.0 (155)	6.5 (119)	6.2 (73)	5.9 (49)	6.8 (13)
Grade 7.....	..	..	10.5 (3)	11.5 (41)	10.1 (115)	9.9 (97)	8.8 (75)	6.5 (17)
Grade 8.....	..	..	19 (1)	13.6 (9)	13.6 (54)	12.3 (146)	11.6 (135)	11.0 (58)

TABLE 11
MEDIANS FOR EACH AGE IN EACH GRADE
CHARACTER B

	8½	9½	10½	11½	12½	13½	14½	15½
Grade 4.....	1.9 (29)	2.2 (173)	1.8 (119)	1.3 (42)	1.3 (23)	1.1 (7)	1.2 (3)	..
Grade 5.....	8.5 (2)	5.9 (23)	4.5 (102)	3.9 (95)	3.3 (44)	3.3 (35)	4.5 (13)	3.3 (9)
Grade 6.....	..	12.5 (2)	8.4 (55)	7.1 (157)	5.8 (116)	5.8 (73)	5.2 (49)	6.3 (13)
Grade 7.....	..	..	9.5 (4)	9.8 (41)	9.5 (115)	9.6 (98)	7.9 (75)	3.9 (17)
Grade 8.....	..	..	10 (1)	14.5 (9)	12.1 (51)	11.3 (146)	10.2 (135)	9.5 (57)

It will be noted that there is a general tendency in all the scales for the younger pupils in any grade to achieve a higher median score than the older pupils of that grade. In the upper grades the younger pupils of one grade tend to achieve as high or even a higher median score than the older pupils of the next higher grade.

It will be noted, too, that in all the scales, despite the fact that the younger pupils in the grade are likely to be promoted more rapidly while the older pupils are more likely to be retarded, the interval between the median achievement of the younger pupils in the fourth grade and the median achievement of the younger pupils in the eighth grade is greater than the interval between the median achievement of the older pupils in the fourth grade and the median achievement of the older pupils in the eighth grade. The younger pupils in the grade not only tend to start with a higher score in the lower grade and to advance more rapidly from grade to grade but they also tend to accomplish more while passing through the grades in a shorter time than the older pupils tend to accomplish while taking a longer time to complete the work of the same grades.

The boys of the schools tested do notably better than the girls in all three of these abilities, especially in the Information Scales. A summary of the facts is given below. The detailed facts are given in Tables 59 to 65 in Appendix II.

TABLE 12

PER CENT OF BOYS EQUALLING OR EXCEEDING THE MEDIAN ACCOMPLISHMENT OF GIRLS IN THE SAME GRADE

	Informa- tion A	Informa- tion B	Thought A	Thought B	Charac- ter A	Charac- ter B	Charac- ter L
Grade 4	74.3	80.6	62.5	67.6	52.9	51.0	45.7
Grade 5	81.9	82.6	74.8	67.6	55.3	57.3	52.0
Grade 6	82.7	82.6	80.6	77.1	60.2	63.8	63.3
Grade 7	89.9	91.0	74.3	79.2	59.1	54.2	64.8
Grade 8	88.6	83.3	78.5	72.4	59.9	61.6	65.8
Average	83.5	84.0	74.1	72.8	57.5	57.6	58.3

TABLE 13

PER CENT OF GIRLS EQUALLING OR EXCEEDING THE MEDIAN ACCOMPLISHMENT OF BOYS IN THE SAME GRADE

	Informa- tion A	Informa- tion B	Thought A	Thought B	Charac- ter A	Charac- ter B	Charac- ter L
Grade 4	24.5	11.9	38.7	25.8	46.9	48.8	55.4
Grade 5	20.1	23.6	30.1	31.9	44.1	42.2	46.3
Grade 6	16.2	19.4	20.5	22.9	43.9	34.3	33.3
Grade 7	8.7	11.6	23.4	25.4	41.7	46.3	33.3
Grade 8	15.0	20.4	23.7	27.6	40.0	39.1	36.6
Average	21.1	21.7	27.3	26.7	43.3	42.1	41.0

In the Thought Scales the per cent of boys who do more problems correctly than the median girl in each grade is less marked than in the case of the Information Scales. The tendency for the per cent of boys excelling the median girl to increase from grade to grade is also present at least up to the seventh grade.

In the Character Scales the per cent of boys who do more problems correctly than the median girl in each grade is still less marked. The tendency for the percentage of boys excelling the median girl to increase from grade to grade up to the seventh grade is evident just as it is in the case of the other scales. The facts given in these tables clearly show the increasing superiority of the boys over the girls in doing these tasks from the fourth grade up to the seventh grade at least, and, in the case of the Information Scales, up to the eighth grade, the greatest superiority being shown in the Information Scales and the least in the Character Scales, where the effect of class-room work is probably least apparent.

INTERCORRELATION OF THE THREE ABILITIES

The correlations in the following tables indicate clearly that information ability—ability to answer correctly questions asking for definite facts—is not antagonistic to or divorced from thought ability, as is sometimes thought, but is closely related to it. To learn facts with an understanding of their meanings requires thought in so far as selective thinking is involved in the perception of the definite relations essential in a comprehension of the meanings. The response in correctly answering an information question which has not become a fixed habit of reaction requires thought in order to interpret the question,—to locate clearly what information is called for—and to reject all inappropriate associations, selecting from the several associations that may be recalled by the various words and phrases of the question or the mental set peculiar to it, that one which actually answers the question. Then, too, an inference depends in a large measure upon the possession of information, either specific or generalized, which has been acquired in situations in which similar elements are probably involved.

In Tables 14, 15, and 16 are given the raw coefficients obtained by correlating the scores of the seventh and eighth grade pupils in each scale with those of every other scale, with the exception of Character Scale L. By using the formula

$$r_{pq} = \frac{\sqrt{(r_{p_1 q_2})\,(r_{p_2 q_1})}}{\sqrt{(r_{p_1 p_2})\,(r_{q_1 q_2})}}$$

to make correction for attenuation, the ability to answer the information questions evidently correlates with the ability to do the thought problems above .80 in the seventh and eighth grades. The next closest relationship is found between the ability to do the thought problems and the ability to do the tasks involved in the Character Scales (.78). The correlation between the ability to answer the information questions and the ability to do the character tasks is a little below .70.

TABLE 14

CORRELATIONS BETWEEN INFORMATION AND THOUGHT SCALES

Scales	Grade	Sex	No.	r
Information A—Thought A	8	Male	115	.466
Information B—Thought B	8	Male	115	.516
Information A—Thought B	8	Male	115	.539
Information B—Thought A	8	Male	115	.483
Information A—Thought A	7	Male	79	.678
Information B—Thought B	7	Male	79	.823
Information A—Thought B	7	Male	79	.662
Information B—Thought A	7	Male	79	.657
Information A—Thought A	8	Female	141	.637
Information B—Thought B	8	Female	141	.611
Information A—Thought B	8	Female	141	.542
Information B—Thought A	8	Female	141	.658
Information A—Thought A	7	Female	111	.476
Information B—Thought B	7	Female	111	.648
Information A—Thought B	7	Female	111	.439
Information B—Thought A	7	Female	111	.731
Information A—Thought A	8	Both	256	.628
Information B—Thought B	8	Both	256	.625
Information A—Thought B	8	Both	256	.592
Information B—Thought A	8	Both	256	.653
Information A—Thought A	7	Both	190	.600
Information B—Thought B	7	Both	190	.757
Information A—Thought B	7	Both	190	.608
Information B—Thought A	7	Both	190	.718

TABLE 15

CORRELATIONS BETWEEN INFORMATION AND CHARACTER SCALES

Scales	Grade	Sex	No.	r
Information A—Character A	8	Male	115	.455
Information B—Character B	8	Male	115	.387
Information A—Character B	8	Male	115	.494
Information B—Character A	8	Male	115	.400
Information A—Character A	7	Male	79	.660
Information B—Character B	7	Male	79	.557
Information A—Character B	7	Male	79	.568
Information B—Character A	7	Male	79	.631
Information A—Character A	8	Female	141	.551
Information B—Character B	8	Female	141	.613
Information A—Character B	8	Female	141	.548
Information B—Character A	8	Female	141	.579

TABLE 15—*Continued*

CORRELATIONS BETWEEN INFORMATION AND CHARACTER SCALES

Scales	Grade	Sex	No.	r
Information A—Character A	7	Female	111	.452
Information B—Character B	7	Female	111	.621
Information A—Character B	7	Female	111	.459
Information B—Character A	7	Female	111	.673
Information A—Character A	8	Both	256	.526
Information B—Character B	8	Both	256	.546
Information A—Character B	8	Both	256	.543
Information B—Character A	8	Both	256	.557
Information A—Character A	7	Both	190	.521
Information B—Character B	7	Both	190	.575
Information A—Character B	7	Both	190	.492
Information B—Character A	7	Both	190	.626

TABLE 16

CORRELATIONS BETWEEN THOUGHT AND CHARACTER SCALES

Scales	Grade	Sex	No.	r
Thought A—Character A	8	Male	115	.596
Thought B—Character B	8	Male	115	.569
Thought A—Character B	8	Male	115	.560
Thought B—Character A	8	Male	115	.531
Thought A—Character A	7	Male	79	.666
Thought B—Character B	7	Male	79	.583
Thought A—Character B	7	Male	79	.529
Thought B—Character A	7	Male	79	.647
Thought A—Character A	8	Female	141	.748
Thought B—Character B	8	Female	141	.668
Thought A—Character B	8	Female	141	.724
Thought B—Character A	8	Female	141	.718
Thought A—Character A	7	Female	111	.617
Thought B—Character B	7	Female	111	.576
Thought A—Character B	7	Female	111	.597
Thought B—Character A	7	Female	111	.613
Thought A—Character A	8	Both	256	.702
Thought B—Character B	8	Both	256	.648
Thought A—Character B	8	Both	256	.674
Thought B—Character A	8	Both	256	.663
Thought A—Character A	7	Both	190	.640
Thought B—Character B	7	Both	190	.578
Thought A—Character B	7	Both	190	.571
Thought B—Character A	7	Both	190	.622

TABLE 17

CORRELATIONS BETWEEN ABILITIES

(r's of previous tables corrected for attenuation)

Scales	Grade	Sex	No.	r
Information and Thought	8	Male	115	.782
Information and Thought	7	Male	79	.845
Information and Thought	8	Female	141	.803
Information and Thought	7	Female	111	.801
Information and Thought	8	Both	256	.822
Information and Thought	7	Both	190	.845

Average within same sex and grade .81±.01

Information and Character	8	Male	115	.620
Information and Character	7	Male	79	.723
Information and Character	8	Female	141	.711
Information and Character	7	Female	111	.768
Information and Character	8	Both	256	.686
Information and Character	7	Both	190	.689

Average within same sex and grade .71±.02

Thought and Character	8	Male	115	.750
Thought and Character	7	Male	79	.720
Thought and Character	8	Female	141	.890
Thought and Character	7	Female	111	.758
Thought and Character	8	Both	256	.839
Thought and Character	7	Both	190	.739

Average within same sex and grade .78±.02

THE DERIVATION OF THE SCALES:
GRADE DISTRIBUTIONS

During the months of May and June, 1916, preliminary tests were given to about twelve hundred children in three public schools of New York City. In only a few instances, however, was it possible to give all the questions to any one group. The easier questions in each series were tried by children in Grades 4 to 8, while the more difficult questions and problems were tried only in the sixth, seventh, and eighth grades.

From the larger lists of questions,—about two hundred for the Information series, one hundred for the Thought series and eighty for the Character series—such questions and problems were selected as tended to decrease in difficulty from grade to grade. These were then arranged in a tentative order of difficulty for each series and paired off in two groups of approximately equal difficulty. A further selection was made from these two groups by eliminating from each group those questions or problems that tended to lower the correlation between the two groups.

The two groups were then put together and rearranged into two further groups, questions of approximately equal difficulty being included in each group. On the basis of this preliminary testing, Information Scales A and B, Thought Scales A and B, and a part of Character Scales A and B were thus constructed. Character Scales A and B were extended to their present form and Character Scale L was constructed on the basis of additional tests given in one of the public schools in New York City during December, 1916, and January, 1917.

During the spring term of 1917 the history scales in their present form were given in five more public schools of New York City, the Information Scales being given during February and March to nearly 2,350[1] pupils in the second half of Grades 4

[1] The exact number of pupils who attempted each scale in each grade is given in Table 23, Section IV.

to 8; the Thought Scales being given during April and May
to nearly 2,050[1] pupils in the second half of Grades 4 to 8; the
Character Scales being given during April and May to nearly
2,000[1] pupils in the second half of Grades 4 to 8. In two of the
five public schools the pupils tried all of the scales. In order to
insure uniformity in the results the tests were all given and scored
by the author and his wife.

The schools selected for the final tests differed widely as far
as the economic and social background of the pupils was concerned. In fact, the differences were as great as one would probably find in any school system, and certainly very, very much
greater than the difference between any two school systems.
Despite these differences, as well as the other differences among
the schools selected, the order of difficulty for the questions is
nearly the same for the different schools, as well as for different
grades within the same school, as is shown below:

r for Information Scale[2] A
$$\begin{cases} \text{in Grade 8 between Schools W and X} = .97 \\ \text{in Grade 6 between Schools W and X} = .97 \\ \text{in School W between Grades 6 and 8} = .96 \\ \text{in School X between Grades 6 and 8} = .95 \end{cases}$$

r for Thought Scale A
$$\begin{cases} \text{in Grade 8 between Schools W and Y} = .90 \\ \text{in Grade 6 between Schools W and Y} = .94 \\ \text{in School W between Grades 6 and 8} = .88 \\ \text{in School Y between Grades 6 and 8} = .88 \end{cases}$$

r for Character Scale A
$$\begin{cases} \text{in Grade 8 between Schools W and Z} = .93 \\ \text{in Grade 6 between Schools W and Z} = .96 \\ \text{in School W between Grades 6 and 8} = .87 \\ \text{in School Z between Grades 6 and 8} = .87 \end{cases}$$

The number of individuals who took the tests is thus sufficient
to give a useful grading of the tasks for difficulty for the kind of
pupils in question. It will be desirable to check through all the
ratings with children from different school systems in different
localities, using different courses of study in history. This can
be done in connection with the practical use of the scales. Even
as they stand, the scales are surely useful. After they have been
used in various places the author hopes to make a final revision
of the ratings of each task for difficulty.

[1] The exact number of pupils who attempted each scale in each grade is
given in Table 23, Section IV.
[2] These coefficients were calculated by the Spearman "Foot-rule" formula.

Administration of the Tests

Inasmuch as the purpose of the work was to arrange a series of questions or problems graded in difficulty and to determine the distance each pupil could reach in these series, rather than to measure the quantity that could be accomplished in a given time, the pupils were given an opportunity to complete their work. One school period of forty-five minutes was adequate for at least 90 per cent of the pupils to complete any one of the scales. Although the pupils who did not finish within the forty-five minutes were in nearly all cases given enough time in which to complete their work, very little was achieved in the extra time allowed, as the more difficult questions were answered correctly almost entirely by the children who did their work quickly and who completed the task somewhat before the end of the period. In most cases the B scale was given during the period immediately following that in which the A scale was given. In cases where the pupils did not have to change rooms at the end of the period the B scales were given out to each pupil as soon as the A scale was finished and handed in. In all cases the pupils handed in their work as soon as it was completed. As soon as the papers for the A scales had been distributed the following directions were given to the pupils, being repeated for the B scale only when the B scale was given in a period that did not at once follow the period in which the A scale was given:

Directions Used in Giving Information Scales A and B

Fill in the blank spaces at the top of the sheets. As soon as you have done this begin answering the questions, writing your answers in the little boxes just beneath the questions. Make your answers brief but clear and definite. For instance, in answering the first question, if you think Columbus found the Chinese in America, write the word "Chinese"; do not take the time to write the sentence: "Columbus found the Chinese in America." Make your answers clear and definite. If, for instance, in answering a question you wish to use the word "boat" and there might be several different kinds of boats, tell whether you mean a steam boat, a row boat or whatever kind of a boat you do mean. Read the questions carefully before answering them. In question 10, for instance, it tells you to "Pick out the thing that you think happened first and put the '1' in front of it," not after it. "Then pick out the thing which happened next and put the '2' in front of it and so on until you have put the '5' in front of the thing which happened last." In question 19, for instance, it asks "Which *one* of these things. . . ?" To put two or three of the things down would, of course, make your answer wrong.

DIRECTIONS USED IN GIVING THOUGHT SCALES A AND B

Fill in the blank spaces at the top of the sheets. In each of the little boxes you will find a paragraph or in some cases two or more paragraphs giving you certain facts. Below the paragraph or paragraphs you will find a question, and in some cases, two or three questions. These are not memory questions; that is, they are not questions to which you are expected to recall an answer which you have learned at some time in the past. Read the paragraph or paragraphs carefully, and from the facts given there think out the answer for yourself. Do not write more than is necessary to make your answer clear and accurate.

DIRECTIONS USED IN GIVING CHARACTER SCALES A AND B

Fill in the blank spaces at the top of the sheet. In each of these boxes you will find one or more paragraphs telling a story. Below the paragraphs in each case you will find a direction similar to this one in question 1,—"Draw a line under the three of the following words which you think best describe the action of these white men." In each question draw a line under those three of the ten words which you think best describe the people who are doing something in the story, or the action of these people, or the character of these people. In each case, underline three words and only three. Your answer cannot be correct if you underline only two words or more than three words.

DIRECTIONS USED IN GIVING CHARACTER SCALE L

Fill in the blank spaces at the top of the sheet. In each of these boxes you will find one or more paragraphs telling a story. Below the paragraphs in each case you will find a direction similar to this one in question 1,—"Put a check mark in front of the three of the following motives which you think were the ones which most likely prompted Elizabeth Zane to go after the powder." When you do something you usually have reasons or motives for doing it. In the same way these people probably had reasons or motives for doing what they did. In each question put a check mark in front of those three of the ten motives which you think most likely prompted the people to do what they did in each story. Put your check marks on the dotted line just in front of the capital letter with which the motive begins.

DISTRIBUTION OF SCORES

In Tables 18 to 21 are given the distribution of the scores made by the pupils in Grades 4 to 8, the scores for Information Scales A and B being combined, those for Thought Scales A and B being combined, and those for Character Scales A and B also being combined. Although the questions and problems vary widely in difficulty, the ability to do each question or problem in any set of scales is rated the same as the ability to do any other question or problem in the same set of scales. In scoring the answers partial credits were given as indicated in the keys to the scales in Section VII. A pupil getting three questions each one-third[1] correct or one question two-thirds correct and another question one-third correct received the same credit as he would if he had done one question completely correct.

Tables 18 to 21 should be read as follows: Table 18—in Grade 4, one pupil out of the 492 pupils did correctly less than one out of the 63 Information questions, three pupils out of the 492 pupils did correctly at least one but less than two out of the 63 Information questions, two pupils out of the 492 pupils did correctly at least two but less than three out of the 63 Information questions. At the bottom of the tables, the median, 9.034, indicates that the median pupil or the 246th pupil of Grade 4 did 9.034 questions correctly. The 25 percentile, 6.75, shows that the 123rd pupil from the bottom, counting 25 per cent of the way through the 492 pupils, did 6.75 questions correctly, while the 75 percentile, 11.727, shows that the 369th pupil from the bottom, counting 75 per cent of the way through the 492 pupils, did 11.727 questions correctly.

[1] Answers scored as one-third or two-thirds correct were in reality very much more than one-third or two-thirds correct.

TABLE 18

DISTRIBUTION OF SCORES IN INFORMATION SCALES A AND B COMBINED

	Grade 4	Grade 5	Grade 6	Grade 7	Grade 8
0—0.9	1				
1—1.9	3				
2—2.9	2				
3	15				
4	22	1			
5	41	2	1		
6	52	4	0	2	
7	49	4	1	0	
8	50	8	3	1	
9	58	19	1	1	
10	49	15	6	0	1
11	22	28	8	7	0
12	28	27	11	6	2
13	28	30	7	8	2
14	16	31	22	12	1
15	11	28	14	9	4
16	11	24	28	17	5
17	7	24	26	14	3
18	4	23	22	18	7
19	2	24	16	16	2
20	5	27	25	15	7
21	3	25	28	13	10
22	0	11	24	16	11
23	2	11	25	14	13
24	1	13	28	13	13
25	1	14	28	20	14
26		7	24	17	16
27		4	31	21	14
28		6	17	16	24
29		3	14	12	26
30		3	16	14	25
31		2	16	16	25
32		1	13	19	25
33		1	9	11	17
34		1	11	11	21
35		2	11	8	20
36			4	17	24
37			1	14	17
38			5	6	20
39			7	5	16
40			2	9	13
41			2	5	13
42			3	2	12
43			2	1	4
44			2	2	9
45			1	4	5
46			1	0	4
47				0	8
48				1	4
49					0
50					2
51					1
52					
53					
54					
55					
56					
57					
58					
59					
60					
61					
62					
63					
No. of pupils	492	423	516	413	460
Median	9.034	16.604	23.600	26.264	32.200
25 percentile	6.750	12.916	18.045	19.515	27.285
75 percentile	11.727	20.935	28.470	32.618	37.764

TABLE 19

Distribution of Scores in Thought Scales A and B Combined

	Grade 4	Grade 5	Grade 6	Grade 7	Grade 8
0—0.9	39				
1—1.9	43				
2—2.9	61		2		
3	74		1	1	1
4	57		5	0	0
5	55		5	0	0
6	47		6	2	0
7	18		7	0	0
8	19		10	6	0
9	10		10	2	1
10	6		15	4	5
11	9		10	6	2
12	5		7	8	0
13	1		10	7	3
14	5		28	7	0
15	1		12	6	4
16	1	3	16	5	5
17	1	25	16	4	3
18	0	8	20	10	0
19	0	6	15	4	6
20	0	8	18	13	8
21	1	5	11	7	7
22	0	4	13	13	14
23	0	5	11	8	3
24	1	5	11	11	10
25		3	13	11	9
26		7	12	18	10
27		0	8	14	4
28		3	21	12	13
29		4	13	14	4
30		2	8	15	15
31		0	10	18	20
32		0	8	14	12
33		0	12	6	16
34		0	8	10	14
35		1	7	7	12
36			6	13	11
37			3	7	18
38			4	9	17
39			6	8	18
40			6	7	14
41			2	4	23
42			3	7	12
43			1	4	19
44			2	7	11
45			2	6	13
46				5	5
47				3	14
48				1	6
49				1	3
50					4
51					4
52					4
53					3
54					1
55					0
56					1
57					
58					
59					
No. of pupils	454	395	414	355	398
Median	4.175	9.944	20.666	28.041	36.181
25 percentile	2.516	6.507	14.553	20.519	28.654
75 percentile	6.244	15.347	28.881	35.035	42.041

TABLE 20

DISTRIBUTION OF SCORES IN CHARACTER SCALES A AND B COMBINED

	Grade 4	Grade 5	Grade 6	Grade 7	Grade 8
0—0.9	27	3	1		
1—1.9	60	8	3		
2—2.9	79	19	5		
3	48	23	7		
4	47	33	9	4	1
5	38	26	27	6	0
6	21	35	26	8	1
7	14	16	20	7	4
8	10	27	30	9	5
9	14	20	22	14	8
10	9	19	32	12	8
11	4	13	33	18	5
12	3	18	18	16	14
13	7	11	26	19	13
14	3	12	20	14	8
15	3	8	22	27	16
16	1	8	19	14	19
17	1	3	16	10	20
18	1	4	19	15	16
19	0	5	12	17	23
20	0	3	11	16	26
21	2	1	19	15	23
22	0	2	12	21	16
23	1	4	9	13	20
24		1	8	10	13
25		3	9	9	22
26		1	8	10	17
27		2	8	10	17
28		0	6	12	16
29		1	1	13	19
30		1	5	11	24
31			4	5	13
32			3	3	11
33			0	3	10
34			1	4	6
35			0	1	6
36			1	2	3
37					
38					
No. of pupils	393	330	472	358	423
Median	3.635	8.074	13.115	18.733	22.093
25 percentile	2.142	4.894	8.666	12.718	17.187
75 percentile	5.888	12.305	18.947	24.350	28.140

TABLE 21

DISTRIBUTION OF SCORES IN CHARACTER SCALE L

	Grade 4	Grade 5	Grade 6	Grade 7	Grade 8
0—0.9	170	63	33	12	2
1—1.9	121	77	59	25	12
2—2.9	65	63	50	40	23
3	24	39	64	46	33
4	10	30	63	32	41
5	7	26	53	31	35
6	1	13	42	35	33
7	1	7	44	31	50
8		6	19	36	48
9		2	12	29	47
10		2	14	26	48
11		2	7	5	31
12		1	4	6	18
13			0		2
14			1		
No. of pupils	399	331	465	354	423
Median	1.243	2.405	4.420	5.709	7.650
25 percentile	.586	1.256	2.485	3.250	4.872
75 percentile	2.127	4.208	6.636	8.375	9.856

MEDIAN ACHIEVEMENT OF EACH GRADE IN EACH SCALE

In Table 22 are given the median achievements of each grade in each scale while in Table 23 are given the number of pupils from whose scores the medians of Table 22 are derived.

TABLE 22

GRADE MEDIANS—BOYS AND GIRLS

Scale	Information A	Information B	Thought A	Thought B	Character A	Character B	Character L
Grade 4	4.895	4.577	2.539	1.902	1.958	1.766	1.243
Grade 5	8.859	8.250	5.473	5.163	4.188	3.981	2.404
Grade 6	11.800	11.872	10.560	10.680	6.914	6.226	4.420
Grade 7	12.464	13.638	14.141	14.103	9.750	8.928	5.709
Grade 8	15.679	16.739	17.571	18.580	11.885	10.678	7.650

TABLE 23

NUMBER OF PUPILS WHO ATTEMPTED EACH SCALE IN EACH GRADE

Scale	Information A	Information B	Thought A	Thought B	Character A	Character B	Character L
Grade 4	499	498	459	457	400	397	399
Grade 5	432	434	400	401	331	332	331
Grade 6	532	527	428	419	472	473	465
Grade 7	426	415	362	360	358	358	354
Grade 8	460	462	404	402	427	426	423
Totals	2,349	2,336	2,053	2,039	1,988	1,986	1,972

Figs. 1 to 15 show graphically the facts given in Tables 18, 19, and 20. The numbers along the base line represent the number of questions or tasks correctly done, while those along the vertical line represent the number of pupils.

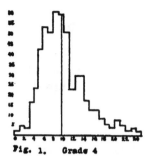

Fig. 1.   Grade 4

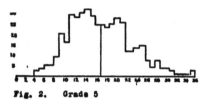

Fig. 2.   Grade 5

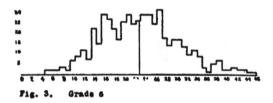

Fig. 3.   Grade 6

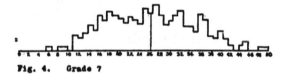

Fig. 4.   Grade 7

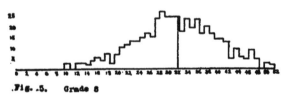

.Fig. .5.   Grade 8

DISTRIBUTION FOR INFORMATION SCALES A AND B COMBINED

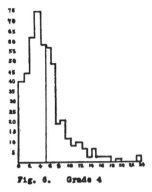

Fig. 6. Grade 4

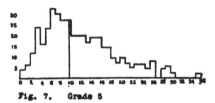

Fig. 7. Grade 5

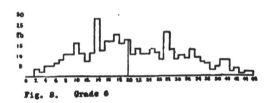

Fig. 8. Grade 6

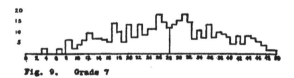

Fig. 9. Grade 7

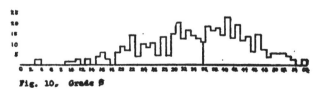

Fig. 10. Grade 8

DISTRIBUTION FOR THE THOUGHT SCALES A AND B COMBINED

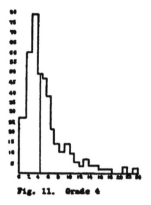

Fig. 11.   Grade 4

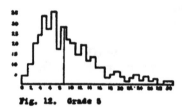

Fig. 12.   Grade 5

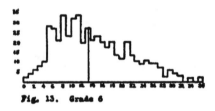

Fig. 13.   Grade 6

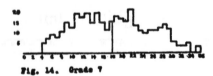

Fig. 14.   Grade 7

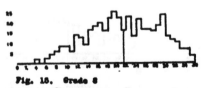

Fig. 15.   Grade 8

DISTRIBUTION FOR THE CHARACTER SCALES A AND B COMBINED

OVERLAPPING AND DIFFERENCE BETWEEN MEDIAN DIFFICULTIES FOR THE DIFFERENT GRADES

It will be noted that wide variability in each grade and extensive overlapping of grades are characteristics of the history scales just as they are of the scales that have been worked out in spelling, language, and arithmetic. Tables 24 to 27 give the number and per cent of pupils in each grade who equal or exceed the achievement of the median pupil in each other grade.

Tables 24 to 27 should be read as follows: Table 24—29 pupils out of 492 pupils, or 5.8 per cent of Grade 4, did as well as or better than the median pupil of Grade 5; 3 pupils out of 492 pupils, or 0.6 per cent of Grade 4, did as well as or better than the median pupil of Grade 6; 403 pupils out of 423 pupils, or 95.2 per cent of Grade 5, did as well as or better than the median pupil of Grade 4; 61 pupils out of 423 pupils, or 14.4 per cent of Grade 5, did as well as or better than the median pupil of Grade 6.

TABLE 24

NUMBER AND PER CENT OF PUPILS IN EACH GRADE WHOSE ABILITY EQUALLED OR EXCEEDED THAT OF THE MEDIAN PUPIL IN EACH OTHER GRADE

Information Scales A and B combined

	Grade 4		Grade 5		Grade 6		Grade 7		Grade 8	
	No.	%	No.	%	No.	%	No.	%	No.	%
Grade 4 (No. = 492) (Med. = 9.034)			29	5.8	3	0.6	0	0.0	0	0.0
Grade 5 (No. = 423) (Med. = 16.604)	403	95.2			61	14.4	28	6.6		1.1
Grade 6 (No. = 516) (Med. = 23.600)	511	99.0	425	82.3			186	36.0	71	13.7
Grade 7 (No. = 413) (Med. = 26.264)	410	99.2	357	86.4	250	60.5			111	26.8
Grade 8 (No. = 460) (Med. = 32.200)	460	100.0	447	97.1	397	86.3	361	78.4		

NUMBER AND PER CENT OF PUPILS IN EACH GRADE WHOSE ABILITY EQUALLED
OR EXCEEDED THAT OF THE MEDIAN PUPIL IN EACH OTHER GRADE

TABLE 25
Thought Scales A and B combined

	Grade 4		Grade 5		Grade 6		Grade 7		Grade 8	
	No.	%	No.	%	No.	%	No.	%	No.	%
Grade 4 (No. = 454) (Med. = 4.175)			32	7.0	2	0.4	0	0.0	0	0.0
Grade 5 (No. = 395) (Med. = 9.944)	348	88.1			42	10.6	10	2.5	)	0.0
Grade 6 (No. = 414) (Med. = 20.666)	410	99.0	369	89.1			121	29.2	34	8.2
Grade 7 (No. = 355) (Med. = 28.041)	354	99.7	344	96.9	264	74.3			80	22.5
Grade 8 (No. = 398) (Med. = 36.181)	397	99.7	396	99.5	367	92.2	306	76.8		

TABLE 26
Character Scales A and B combined

	Grade 4		Grade 5		Grade 6		Grade 7		Grade 8	
	No.	%	No.	%	No.	%	No.	%	No.	%
Grade 4 (No. = 393) (Med. = 3.635)			58	14.7	18	4.5	3	0.7	1	0.2
Grade 5 (No. = 330) (Med. = 8.074)	285	86.3			69	20.9	25	7.5	15	4.5
Grade 6 (No. = 472) (Med. = 13.115)	459	97.2	372	78.8			122	25.8	74	15.6
Grade 7 (No. = 358) (Med. = 18.733)	358	100.0	332	92.7	262	73.1			125	34.9
Grade 8 (No. = 423) (Med. = 22.093)	423	100.0	417	98.5	376	88.8	289	68.3		

TABLE 27
Character Scale L

	Grade 4		Grade 5		Grade 6		Grade 7		Grade 8	
	No.	%	No.	%	No.	%	No.	%	No.	%
Grade 4 (No. = 399) (Med. = 1.243)			82	20.5	15	3.7	4	1.0	0	0.0
Grade 5 (No. = 331) (Med. = 2.404)	249	75.2			76	22.9	41	12.3	15	4.5
Grade 6 (No. = 465) (Med. = 4.420)	418	89.9	353	75.9			158	33.9	72	15.4
Grade 7 (No. = 354) (Med. = 5.709)	336	94.9	301	85.0	218	61.5			113	31.9
Grade 8 (No. = 423) (Med. = 7.650)	418	98.8	400	94.5	336	79.4	287	67.8		

Assuming that these scales are reasonably valid means of measuring the three kinds of ability selected for this study, Figs. 1 to 15 show that these abilities conform closely to the general characteristics of the normal surface of frequency given in Fig. 16.

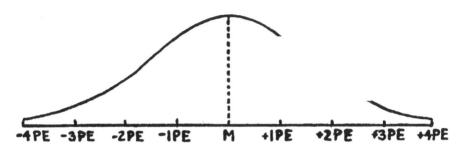

FIG. 16. NORMAL SURFACE OF FREQUENCY, WITH P.E. DISTANCES FROM THE MEDIAN

On the basis of this conformity, then, we may use the P.E. from the median as a unit of measurement of the variability. The P.E., or median deviation, or semi-interquartile range, is the distance cut off on the base line of the normal surface of frequency by one half or 25 per cent of the cases lying on either side of the median (M in Fig. 16). Since the curve tapers toward the extremes the percentage of cases cut off by the distance 1 P.E. decreases toward the extremes:

> 25% of the cases lying between the median, M, and 1 P.E.
> 41.13% of the cases lying between the median, M, and 2 P.E.
> 47.85% of the cases lying between the median, M, and 3 P.E.
> 49.65% of the cases lying between the median, M, and 4 P.E.

Table 28, taken directly from Dr. Buckingham's *Spelling Ability—Its Measurement and Distribution*, shows the amount of each per cent from 0.1 per cent to 49.9 per cent expressed in terms of P.E. This table is worked out on the basis of the frequency table given by Professor Edward L. Thorndike in *Mental and Social Measurements*, which is derived in turn from the fundamental table by W. F. Sheppard.

TABLE 28

P.E. VALUES CORRESPONDING TO GIVEN PER CENTS OF THE NORMAL SURFACE OF FREQUENCY, PER CENTS BEING TAKEN FROM THE MEDIAN

	0	.1	.2	.3	.4	.5	.6	.7	.8	.9
0	.000	.004	.007	.011	.015	.019	.022	.026	.030	.033
1	.037	.041	.044	.048	.052	.056	.059	.063	.067	.071
2	.074	.078	.082	.085	.089	.093	.097	.100	.104	.108
3	.112	.115	.119	.123	.127	.130	.134	.138	.141	.145
4	.149	.153	.156	.160	.164	.168	.172	.175	.179	.183
5	.187	.190	.194	.198	.201	.205	.209	.213	.216	.220
6	.224	.228	.231	.235	.239	.243	.246	.250	.254	.258
7	.261	.265	.269	.273	.277	.280	.284	.288	.292	.296
8	.299	.303	.307	.311	.315	.318	.322	.326	.330	.334
9	.337	.341	.345	.349	.353	.357	.360	.364	.368	.372
10	.376	.380	.383	.387	.391	.395	.399	.403	.407	.410
11	.414	.418	.422	.426	.430	.434	.437	.441	.445	.449
12	.453	.457	.461	.464	.468	.472	.476	.480	.484	.489
13	.492	.496	.500	.504	.508	.512	.516	.519	.523	.527
14	.531	.535	.539	.543	.547	.551	.555	.559	.563	.567
15	.571	.575	.579	.583	.588	.592	.596	.600	.603	.608
16	.612	.616	.620	.624	.628	.632	.636	.640	.644	.648
17	.652	.656	.660	.665	.669	.673	.677	.681	.685	.689
18	.693	.698	.702	.706	.710	.714	.719	.723	.727	.731
19	.735	.740	.744	.748	.752	.756	.761	.765	.769	.773
20	.778	.782	.786	.790	.795	.799	.803	.807	.812	.816
21	.820	.825	.829	.834	.838	.842	.847	.851	.855	.860
22	.864	.869	.873	.878	.882	.886	.891	.895	.900	.904
23	.909	.913	.918	.922	.927	.931	.936	.940	.945	.949
24	.954	.958	.963	.968	.972	.977	.982	.986	.991	.996
25	1.000	1.005	1.009	1.014	1.019	1.024	1.028	1.033	1.038	1.042
26	1.047	1.052	1.057	1.062	1.067	1.071	1.076	1.081	1.086	1.091
27	1.096	1.101	1.105	1.110	1.115	1.120	1.125	1.130	1.135	1.140
28	1.145	1.150	1.155	1.160	1.165	1.170	1.176	1.181	1.186	1.191
29	1.196	1.201	1.206	1.211	1.217	1.222	1.227	1.232	1.238	1.243
30	1.248	1.253	1.259	1.264	1.269	1.275	1.279	1.286	1.291	1.296
31	1.302	1.307	1.313	1.318	1.324	1.329	1.335	1.340	1.346	1.351
32	1.357	1.363	1.368	1.374	1.380	1.386	1.391	1.397	1.403	1.409
33	1.415	1.421	1.427	1.432	1.438	1.444	1.450	1.456	1.462	1.469
34	1.475	1.481	1.487	1.493	1.499	1.506	1.512	1.518	1.524	1.531
35	1.537	1.543	1.549	1.556	1.563	1.569	1.576	1.582	1.589	1.595
36	1.602	1.609	1.616	1.622	1.629	1.636	1.643	1.649	1.656	1.663
37	1.670	1.677	1.685	1.692	1.699	1.706	1.713	1.720	1.728	1.735
38	1.742	1.749	1.757	1.765	1.772	1.780	1.788	1.795	1.803	1.811
39	1.819	1.827	1.835	1.843	1.851	1.859	1.867	1.875	1.884	1.892
40	1.900	1.909	1.918	1.926	1.935	1.944	1.953	1.962	1.971	1.979
41	1.988	1.997	2.007	2.016	2.026	2.035	2.044	2.054	2.064	2.074
42	2.083	2.093	2.103	2.114	2.124	2.134	2.145	2.155	2.166	2.177
43	2.188	2.199	2.211	2.222	2.234	2.245	2.257	2.269	2.281	2.293
44	2.305	2.318	2.331	2.344	2.357	2.370	2.384	2.397	2.411	2.425
45	2.439	2.453	2.468	2.483	2.498	2.514	2.530	2.546	2.562	2.579
46	2.597	2.614	2.631	2.648	2.667	2.686	2.706	2.726	2.746	2.767
47	2.789	2.811	2.834	2.857	2.881	2.905	2.932	2.958	2.986	3.015
48	3.044	3.077	3.111	3.146	3.182	3.219	3.258	3.300	3.346	3.395
49	3.450	3.506	3.571	3.643	3.725	3.820	3.938	4.083	4.275	4.600
50										

Tables 29 to 32 show the percentage of pupils whose ability lay between the median of each grade and that of each other grade with the P.E. values corresponding to each per cent. These tables should be read as follows: Table 29—there are 44.2 per cent of the fourth grade pupils whose ability in the Information Scales is equal to or greater than the ability of the median pupil of the fourth grade and only equal to or less than the ability of the median pupil of the fifth grade. This corresponds to a distance of 2.331 P.E. between the median of the fourth grade and that of the fifth grade. There are 49.4 per cent of the fourth grade pupils whose ability in the Information Scales is equal to or greater than the ability of the median pupil of the fourth grade and only equal to or less than the ability of the median pupil of the sixth grade. This corresponds to a distance of 3.725 P.E. between the median of the fourth grade and that of the sixth grade. There are 45.2 per cent of the fifth grade pupils whose ability in the Information Scales is equal to or greater than the ability of the median pupil of the fourth grade and only equal to or less than the ability of the median pupil of the fifth grade. This corresponds to a distance of—2.468 P.E. between the fifth grade median and that of the fourth grade.

The P.E. distances between the grade medians are determined on the basis of the per cent of pupils whose ability lies between the grade medians in question. Referring to Table 28, it will be seen that the 44.2 per cent lying between the median of Grade 4 and the median of Grade 5 corresponds to 2.331 P.E. while the 45.2 per cent lying between the median of Grade 5 and the median of Grade 4 corresponds to 2.468 P.E.

TABLE 29

PER CENT OF PUPILS WHOSE ABILITY LAY BETWEEN THE MEDIAN OF EACH GRADE AND THAT OF EACH OTHER GRADE, WITH THE P.E. VALUES CORRESPONDING TO EACH PER CENT

Information Scales A and B combined

	Grade 4		Grade 5		Grade 6		Grade 7		Grade 8	
	%	P.E.	%	P.E.	%	P.E.	%	P.E.	%	P.E
Grade 4			44.2	2.331	49.4	3.725				
Grade 5	45.2	−2.468			35.6	1.576	43.4	2.234	48.9	3.395
Grade 6	49.0	−3.450	32.3	−1.374			14.0	0.531	36.3	1.622
Grade 7	49.2	−3.571	36.4	−1.629	10.5	−0.395			23.2	0.918
Grade 8			47.1	−2.811	36.3	−1.622	28.4	−1.165		

TABLE 30

PER CENT OF PUPILS WHOSE ABILITY LAY BETWEEN THE MEDIAN OF EACH GRADE AND THAT OF EACH OTHER GRADE, WITH THE P.E. VALUES CORRESPONDING TO EACH PER CENT

Thought Scales A and B combined

	Grade 4		Grade 5		Grade 6		Grade 7		Grade 8	
	%	P.E.	%	P.E.	%	P.E.	%	P.E.	%	P.E.
Grade 4			43.0	2.188	49.6	3.938				
Grade 5	38.1	−1.749			39.4	1.851	47.5	2.905		
Grade 6	49.0	−3.450	39.1	−1.827			20.8	0.812	41.8	2.064
Grade 7	49.7	−4.083	46.9	−2.767	24.3	−0.968			27.5	1.120
Grade 8	49.7	−4.083	49.5	−3.820	42.2	−2.103	26.8	−1.086		

TABLE 31

PER CENT OF PUPILS WHOSE ABILITY LAY BETWEEN THE MEDIAN OF EACH GRADE AND THAT OF EACH OTHER GRADE, WITH THE P.E. VALUES CORRESPONDING TO EACH PER CENT

Character Scales A and B combined

	Grade 4		Grade 5		Grade 6		Grade 7		Grade 8	
	%	P.E.	%	P.E.	%	P.E.	%	P.E.	%	P.E.
Grade 4			35.3	1.556	45.5	2.514	49.3	3.643		
Grade 5	36.3	−1.622			29.1	1.201	42.5	2.134	45.5	2.514
Grade 6	47.2	−2.834	28.8	−1.186			24.2	0.963	34.4	1.499
Grade 7			42.7	−2.155	23.1	−0.913			15.1	0.575
Grade 8			48.5	−3.219	38.8	−1.803	18.3	−0.706		

TABLE 32

PER CENT OF PUPILS WHOSE ABILITY LAY BETWEEN THE MEDIAN OF EACH GRADE AND THAT OF EACH OTHER GRADE, WITH THE P.E. VALUES CORRESPONDING TO EACH PER CENT

Character Scale L

	Grade 4		Grade 5		Grade 6		Grade 7		Grade 8	
	%	P.E.	%	P.E.	%	P.E.	%	P.E.	%	P.E.
Grade 4			29.5	1/222	46.3	2.648	49.0	3.450		
Grade 5	25.2	−1.009			27.1	1.101	37.7	1.720	45.5	2.514
Grade 6	39.9	−1.892	25.9	−1.042			16.1	0.616	34.6	1.512
Grade 7	44.9	−2.425	35.0	−1.537	11.5	−0.434			18.1	0.698
Grade 8	48.8	−3.346	44.5	−2.370	29.4	−1.217	17.8	−0.685		

On the basis of the assumptions that the abilities measured are normally distributed and that the grades are equal in the variability of the abilities concerned, we should expect to find but a small variability in the distances between grades whether measured by the direct distances or the more remote distances. Inasmuch, however, as the direct distances are likely to show the least variability it would seem that they should be given the most weight. The same system of weighting has been adopted as that used by Dr. B. R. Buckingham in *Spelling Ability—Its Measurement and Distribution*, page 39. The very small difference between the average of the direct and indirect measures and the average of the same measures when weighted shows that the system of weighting selected is of very little moment.

Tables 33 to 36 give both the direct and the indirect distances between the grade medians, together with the average of these distances and the weighted average. These tables should be read as follows: Table 33—the direct distance between the fourth grade median and the fifth grade median is 2.331 P.E., the direct distance between the fifth grade median and the fourth grade median is 2.468 P.E., the indirect distance between the fourth grade median and the fifth grade median, found by subtracting the distance between the fifth grade median and the sixth grade median, 1.576 P.E., from the distance between the fourth grade median and the sixth grade median, 3.725 P.E., is 2.149 P.E., the indirect distance between the fifth grade median and the fourth grade median, found by subtracting the distance between the sixth grade median and the fifth grade median, 1.374 P.E., from the distance between the sixth grade median and the fourth grade median, 3.450 P.E., is 2.076 P.E.

The weighted average is found by giving the two direct distances a weight of six each and the two indirect distances a weight of four each. The indirect distances found from the next wider interval, 4–7—5–7 and 7–4—7–5, would be given a weight of three each, while those found from the widest interval, 4–8—5–8 and 8–4—8–5, would be given a weight of only one each.

TABLE 33
DIRECT AND DERIVED VALUES OF MEDIAN DISTANCES IN TERMS OF P.E.
Information Scales A and B combined

Grade 4–5		Grade 5–6		Grade 6–7		Grade 7–8	
4–5	2.331	5–6	1.576	6–7	.531	7–8	.918
5–4	2.468	6–5	1.374	7–6	1.395	8–7	1.165
4–6—5–6	2.149	4–6—4–5	1.394	4–7—4–6		4–8—4–7	
6–4—6–5	2.076	6–4—5–4	.982	7–4—6–4		8–4—7–4	
4–7—5–7		5–7—6–7	1.703	5–7—5–6	.658	5–8—5–7	1.161
7–4—7–5		7–5—7–6	1.234	7–5—6–5	.255	8–5—7–5	1.182
4–8—5–8		5–8—6–8	1.773	6–8—7–8	.704	6–8—6–7	1.091
8–4—8–5		8–5—8–6	1.189	8–6—8–7	.457	8–6—7–6	1.227
Average	2.256		1.403		.500		1.124
Weighted Average	2.284		1.407		.494		1.107

TABLE 34
DIRECT AND DERIVED VALUES OF MEDIAN DISTANCES IN TERMS OF P.E.
Thought Scales A and B combined

Grade 4–5		Grade 5–6		Grade 6–7		Grade 7–8	
4–5	2.188	5–6	1.851	6–7	.812	7–8	1.120
5–4	1.749	6–5	1.827	7–6	.968	8–7	1.086
4–6—5–6	2.087	4–6—4–5	1.727	4–7—4–6		4–8—4–7	
6–4—6–5	1.623	6–4—5–4	1.722	7–4—6–4		8–4—7–4	
4–7—5–7		5–7—6–7	2.093	5–7—5–6	1.054	5–8—5–7	
7–4—7–5		7–5—7–6	1.799	7–5—6–5	.940	8–5—7–5	
4–8—5–8		5–8—6–8		6–8—7–8	.944	6–8—6–7	1.252
8–4—8–5		8–5—8–6		8–6—8–7	1.017	8–6—7–6	1.135
Average	1.912		1.836		.955		1.148
Weighted Average	1.923		1.836		.946		1.139

TABLE 35
Direct and Derived Values of Median Distances in Terms of P.E.
Character Scales A and B combined

Grade 4–5		Grade 5–6		Grade 6–7		Grade 7–8	
4–5	1.556	5–6	1.201	6–7	.963	7–8	.575
5–4	1.622	6–5	1.186	7–6	.913	8–7	.706
4–6—5–6	1.313	4–6—4–5	.958	4–7—4–6		4–8—4–7	
6–4—6–5	1.648	6–4—5–4	1.212	7–4—6–4		8–4—7–4	
4–7—5–7		5–7—6–7	1.171	5–7—5–6	.933	5–8—5–7	.380
7–4—7–5		7–5—7–6	1.242	7–5—6–5	.969	8–5—7–5	1.064
4–8—5–8		5–8—6–8	1.015	6–8—7–8	.924	6–8—6–7	.536
8–4—8–5		8–5—8–6	1.416	8–6—8–7	1.097	8–6—7–6	.890
Average	1.534		1.175		.966		.691
Weighted Average	1.545		1.174		.962		.681

TABLE 36
Direct and Derived Values of Median Distances in Terms of P.E.
Character Scale L

Grade 4–5		Grade 5–6		Grade 6–7		Grade 7–8	
4–5	1.222	5–6	1.101	6–7	.616	7–8	.698
5–4	1.009	6–5	1.042	7–6	.434	8–7	.685
4–6—5–6	1.547	4–6—4–5	1.426	4–7—4–6	.802	4–8—4–7	
6–4—6–5	.850	6–4—5–4	.883	7–4—6–4	.533	8–4—7–4	
4–7—5–7	1.730	5–7—6–7	1.104	5–7—5–6	.619	5–8—5–7	.794
7–4—7–5	.888	7–5—7–6	1.103	7–5—6–5	.495	8–5—7–5	.833
4–8—5–8		5–8—6–8	1.002	6–8—7–8	.814	6–8—6–7	.896
8–4—8–5		8–5—8–6	1.153	8–6—8–7	.532	8–6—7–6	.783
Average	1.207		1.101		.607		.781
Weighted Average	1.185		1.099		.592		.765

It will be noted that in all the scales the largest grade interval falls between Grades 4 and 5, the second largest grade interval falls between Grades 5 and 6, while the smallest grade interval, with the exception of Character Scales A and B combined, falls between Grades 6 and 7. The increase in the grade interval between the seventh and eighth grades may be accounted for in part at least by the extra effort that is put forth by many of the eighth grade pupils to pass the examinations for graduation, the emphasis in the class work probably being mainly placed on such subject matter as would show the greatest influence in the Information Scale and Thought Scale results.

MEASURING THE DIFFICULTY OF EACH QUESTION OR TASK

Tables 37 to 43 give the per cent of pupils in each grade who correctly answered each question or problem in the seven scales. These tables are read as follows: Table 37—in Grade 4, 86.3 per cent of the 499 pupils tested correctly answered question 1 of Information Scale A; in Grade 5, 97.7 per cent of the 432 pupils tested correctly answered question 1 of Information Scale A.

TABLE 37

PER CENT OF PUPILS WHO ANSWERED EACH QUESTION CORRECTLY

Information A

	Grade 4 No. = 499	Grade 5 No. = 432	Grade 6 No. = 532	Grade 7 No. = 426	Grade 8 No. = 460
1	86.3	97.7	96.4	98.5	98.4
2	82.3	90.7	96.8	96.9	98.2
3	77.3	91.4	90.7	91.0	93.4
4	46.1	60.1	85.5	87.3	96.0
5	50.1	78.2	80.8	77.9	70.4
6	14.8	34.9	58.4	82.8	92.1
7	31.8	81.9	81.2	86.8	90.4
8	11.2	38.8	73.8	73.2	71.7
9	19.0	47.4	58.2	67.3	72.8
10	9.1	30.2	41.2	52.8	66.7
11	1.9	11.0	52.7	46.1	66.3
12	16.6	50.0	37.2	43.6	56.5
13	1.0	8.5	68.6	38.9	66.5
14	1.8	38.1	34.6	39.2	49.3
15	0.8	10.6	29.8	30.5	43.4
16	17.4	32.8	56.5	69.9	84.7
17	0.4	52.0	35.3	36.1	54.5
18	[1]	1.8	4.2	24.3	40.5
19	6.4	18.2	20.4	24.8	35.4
20	0.4	1.6	3.5	5.3	9.3
21	[1]	0.5	9.3	17.1	31.4
22	[1]	0.4	18.6	11.5	23.2
23	0.2	0.7	6.0	5.8	18.2
24	[1]	0.0	0.0	0.0	4.3
25	[1]	0.6	15.6	11.1	22.4
26	0.2	1.3	7.5	7.7	17.6
27	[2]	[2]	0.4	1.2	6.5
28	[2]	[2]	12.9	22.9	44.3
29	-	-	3.4	5.0	8.4
30			7.0	4.7	15.6
33			0.4	0.2	2.8
34	[2]	[2]	0.05	0.0	0.7

[1] Indicates that no pupils in the grade answered the question correctly.
[2] Indicates that the question was not tried by the grade.

TABLE 38

PER CENT OF PUPILS WHO ANSWERED EACH QUESTION CORRECTLY
Information B

	Grade 4 No. = 498	Grade 5 No. = 434	Grade 6 No. = 527	Grade 7 No. = 415	Grade 8 No. = 462
1	94.5	99.7	99.4	99.0	99.7
2	90.3	89.6	97.9	98.3	98.2
3	37.7	80.4	69.9	83.8	85.1
4	54.2	59.9	78.1	87.2	95.6
5	32.1	60.1	83.3	79.5	90.9
6	24.3	49.7	82.5	71.6	88.0
7	35.6	63.2	61.8	62.7	70.7
8	29.3	26.9	75.5	63.3	83.5
10	1.2	73.2	62.9	76.3	78.1
11	3.2	26.5	85.5	86.0	94.8
12	1.2	32.9	29.2	48.6	54.5
13	1.8	11.2	33.0	51.0	74.8
14	0.2	23.8	24.2	39.1	57.0
15	21.0	38.4	58.1	70.8	83.3
16	5.6	18.8	33.7	46.8	56.9
17	1.8	10.8	26.3	25.0	37.5
18	[1]	0.4	33.0	48.6	47.8
19	3.8	6.4	17.0	36.1	38.3
20	[1]	[1]	6.4	21.0	44.5
21	[1]	10.9	9.5	16.2	30.8
22	4.0	21.1	25.8	28.1	31.1
23	[1]	[1]	3.7	2.1	2.8
24	0.3	0.9	6.4	12.8	22.2
25	0.6	11.1	25.4	34.2	50.5
26	0.1	0.4	16.5	7.1	22.9
27	[2]	[2]	6.2	14.9	37.0
28	[2]	?	12.3	21.6	38.2
29	^	^	15.0	11.7	24.9
30			1.1	1.2	13.2
33			0.05	0.2	1.0
34			3.0	3.2	8.0

TABLE 39

PER CENT OF PUPILS WHO ANSWERED EACH QUESTION CORRECTLY
Thought A

	Grade 4 No. = 459	Grade 5 No. = 400	Grade 6 No. = 428	Grade 7 No. = 362	Grade 8 No. = 404
1	55.1	72.7	73.8	78.	87.8
2	62.8	72.5	80.9	87	91.8
3	32.1	58.9	64.7	69	80.1
4	26.3	45.0	57.7	67.	72.2
5a	2.6	18.2	41.3	54	72.5
5b	4.5	20.5	60.7	78	83.8
5c	6.3	31.0	67.7	84	91.5
6	[1]	13.8	52.7	51	67.8
7	14.0	25.4	41.0	54	60.9
8	0.5	17.4	42.0	45	62.7
10a	[1]	1.0	2.5	7	19.5
10b	2.8	15.7	43.9	53	74.2
10c	0.2	5.9	22.9	37	63.1
11a	2.2	17.1	52.3	64	75.0

TABLE 39—*Continued*

PER CENT OF PUPILS WHO ANSWERED EACH QUESTION CORRECTLY

Thought A

	Grade 4 No. = 459	Grade 5 No. = 400	Grade 6 No. = 428	Grade 7 No. = 362	Grade 8 No. = 404
11b	0.3	6.0	29.9	41	53.8
12	17.9	28	45	57	75.
13	.	29.	41	48	63
14	.	.	55	55	58
15a	.	.	13	40	49
15b	.	.	2	20	19
16a	.	.	41	25	66
16b	-	.	20		47
17		.	14		28
18		.	22		35
19		.	28	5	51
20a		.	13		34
20b		.	11		35
21		.	22		43
22		.	7		37

TABLE 40

PER CENT OF PUPILS WHO ANSWERED EACH QUESTION CORRECTLY

Thought B

	Grade 4 No. = 457	Grade 5 No. = 401	Grade 6 No. = 419	Grade 7 No. = 360	Grade 8 No. = 402
1	68	80.8	83.5	96.3	98.3
2a	44	83.	89	90.2	94.5
2b	37	69	1	78.8	80.5
3a	6	7	4	46.1	65.6
3b	5	18	1	63.8	80.6
3c	2	8.	40.0	61.1	8.3
4	13	41	59.5	68.0	68.4
5	4	19	62.5	60.5	76.1
6	1	6	71.8	53.0	73.3
7a	2	11.	30.7	1.8	7.1
7b	6	31	63.3	5.6	8.8
8	1	21	46.7	50.8	64.1
9	3	18.	51.6	62.9	72.6
10	5	19	36.5	38.3	46.7
11	1	4.	8.3	27.5	3.0
12a	3	12	35.4	46.2	66.2
12b	0.	6	20.6	38.2	57.7
13a	2	28.	50.1	68.4	78.6
13b	1	13	25.7	3.0	5.2
14a	1	0	1.9	.2	1.9
14b	1.7	9	27.9	4.6	7.3
15	3.8	16	34.5	8.4	6.3
16	2	2.	3.6	7	33.5
17	2	2.	5.9	.2	55.3
18	-	2	1.9	.8	28.0
19		1	6.2	.5	37.8
20a		11	41.6	.5	68.5
20b		1	5.0	.1	1.1
21		1	4.1	.3	1.9
22		0	2.5	.6	6

TABLE 41

PER CENT OF PUPILS WHO ANSWERED EACH QUESTION CORRECTLY
Character A

	Grade 4 No. = 400	Grade 5 No. = 331	Grade 6 No. = 472	Grade 7 No. = 358	Grade 8 No. = 427
1	33.8	54.2	65.6	76.2	75.3
2	32.0	50.7	67.9	75.5	83.0
3	34.0	45.2	54.6	62.9	64.2
4	10.2	18.5	38.7	50.9	64.0
5	28.4	56.2	78.1	87.9	70.6
6a	15.5	25.6	44.5	54.8	67.9
6b	18.0	26.1	48.4	63.5	72.7
7a	8.5	24.9	45.4	62.2	73.3
7b	10.8	22.2	35.5	45.5	56.9
8	12.9	23.9	43.5	58.3	67.1
9	19.6	38.1	63.0	68.5	81.1
10	16.5	26.0	33.5	45.6	58.4
11	3.2	8.5	20.4	36.7	50.0
12	a	8.1	19.5	34.0	51.2
13a	a	9.7	27.2	43.2	56.6
13b	a	6.3	15.0	26.3	40.9
14		3.3	14.5	25.0	43.8
15a		7.8	19.0	29.7	34.8
15b		6.0	14.6	23.3	38.0

TABLE 42

PER CENT OF PUPILS WHO ANSWERED EACH QUESTION CORRECTLY
Character B

	Grade 4 No. = 397	Grade 5 No. = 332	Grade 6 No. = 473	Grade 7 No. = 358	Grade 8 No. = 426
1	34.0	59.7	78.2	86.3	91.6
2a	10.5	20.8	39.3	57.9	68.7
2b	20.9	32.9	57.7	73.4	77.8
3	29.8	36.5	48.9	54.2	60.7
4	8.9	22.4	39.6	54.1	62.8
5a	14.6	29.4	41.9	59.5	67.6
5b	15.3	37.6	55.9	70.4	78.8
6	36.4	62.9	71.9	81.5	87.4
7	5.3	11.0	24.1	38.1	54.8
8a	13.0	26.5	29.7	42.7	52.1
8b	3.0	6.5	16.7	35.0	46.8
8c	10.9	17.0	20.7	31.4	45.1
9	a	27.4	41.7	52.7	64.9
10	a	16.1	33.5	52.7	64.0
11	a	3.7	9.0	17.0	23.0
12		17.4	22.1	36.9	39.7
13a		9.5	13.5	29.7	30.4
13b		7.4	9.7	14.7	16.2
14		1.9	3.7	6.7	13.2

By making use of a reasonable assumption we now turn these measures of difficulty of Tables 37 to 43 in terms of the per cent of successes into measures in terms of deviation up or down from the median difficulty for the grade in question, the assumption being that the form of distribution of ability within any one

TABLE 43

PER CENT OF PUPILS WHO ANSWERED EACH QUESTION CORRECTLY

Character L

	Grade 4 No. = 399	Grade 5 No. = 331	Grade 6 No. = 465	Grade 7 No. = 354	Grade 8 No. = 423
1	26.8	42.5	63.8	72.5	76.9
2	39.7	50.3	67.0	71.4	74.3
3a	13.8	20.8	30.9	41.2	50.2
3b	10.1	23.3	37.2	44.2	56.5
4	15.5	19.2	29.3	38.4	47.2
5	13.1	16.0	33.7	42.0	52.9
6	16.2	22.7	36.0	50.5	58.3
7a	2	21.6	38.5	48.9	67.0
7b	2	6.5	14.7	20.9	3 .2
8a	.	14.4	29.2	38.3	5 .1
8b		7.7	13.9	19.6	3 .8
9a		9.6	18.7	28.7	4 .1
9b		10.6	18.4	23.3	3 .0
10		13.4	24.2	29.5	40.0

grade is symmetrical and approximately that of the normal probability surface. The method is the familiar one used by Dr. Buckingham. The result is a series of tables of which the one for the Information Scale A is given here as a sample. This table (44) should be read as follows: In Grade 4 question 1 of Information Scale A is 1.622 P.E. below the fourth grade median, in Grade 5 it is 2.958 P.E. below the fifth grade median, in Grade 6 it is 2.667 P.E. below the sixth grade median, in Grade 7 it is 3.219 P.E. below the seventh grade median, in Grade 8 it is 3.182 below the eighth grade median.

We may now refer all the tasks of one test to one point and place them in relation one to another in the same scale by making one further assumption: namely, that the grades (4, 5, 6, 7, and 8) are approximately equal in variability in respect to the ability in question. This assumption is almost certainly somewhat in error; but it is perhaps more nearly true than any other single relation that would be suggested. It, therefore, may serve for a first approximation. It has the additional merit that it is the assumption which has been used for similar scales in other subjects. The median difficulty for fourth grade pupils is the arbitrary point of reference used here.

In Tables 47 to 53 are given the distances in terms of P.E. of each question or problem above the fourth grade median difficulty, first when the data of each grade in which it was given are used separately, and, finally, when all data available are combined into a single estimate. These tables should be read

4

TABLE 44

P.E. VALUES OF EACH QUESTION

Information A

	Grade 4	Grade 5	Grade 6	Grade 7	Grade 8
1	−1.622	−2.958	−2.667	−3.219	−3.182
2	−1.374	−1.962	−2.746	−2.767	−3.111
3	−1.110	−2.026	−1.962	−1.988	−2.234
4	+0.145	−0.380	−1.569	−1.692	−2.597
5	−0.004	−1.155	−1.291	−1.140	−0.795
6	+1.549	+0.575	−0.315	−1.403	−2.093
7	+0.702	−1.351	−1.313	−1.656	−1.935
8	+1.803	+0.422	−0.945	−0.913	−0.851
9	+1.302	+0.097	−0.307	−0.665	−0.900
10	+1.979	+0.769	+0.330	−0.104	−0.640
11	+3.077	+0.819	−0.100	+0.145	−0.624
12	+1.438	0.000	+0.484	+0.235	−0.242
13	+3.450	+2.035	−0.719	+0.418	−0.632
14	+3.111	+0.449	+0.588	+0.407	+0.026
15	+3.571	+1.851	+0.786	+0.756	+0.246
16	+1.391	+0.660	−0.243	−0.773	−1.518
17	+3.938	−0.074	+0.559	+0.527	−0.168
18	[1]	+3.111	+2.562	+1.033	+0.357
19	+2.257	+1.346	+1.227	+1.009	+0.555
20	+3.938	+3.182	+2.686	+2.397	+1.962
21	[1]	+3.820	+1.962	+1.409	+0.719
22	[1]	+3.938	+1.324	+1.780	+1.086
23	+4.275	+3.643	+2.305	+2.331	+1.346
24	[1]	[1]	[1]	[1]	+2.546
25	[1]	+3.643	+1.499	+1.811.	+1.125
26	+4.275	+3.300	+2.134	+2.114	+1.380
27	[2]	[2]	+3.938	+3.346	+2.245
28	[2]	[2]	+1.677	+1.101	+0.213
29	-	-	+2.706	+2.439	+2.044
30	.	.	+2.188	+2.344	+1.499
33			+3.938	+4.275	+2.834
34	[2]	[2]	[2]	[2]	+3.643

[1] Indicates that no pupils in the grade answered the question correctly.
[2] Indicates that the question was not tried by the grade.

as follows: Table 47—on the basis of the results obtained in Grade 4, question 1 of Information Scale A lies 1.622 P.E. below the fourth grade median; on the basis of the results obtained in Grade 5, it lies .674 P.E. below the fourth grade median; on the basis of the results obtained in Grade 6, it lies 1.024 P.E. above the fourth grade median; on the basis of the results obtained in Grade 7, it lies .968 P.E. above the fourth grade median; on the basis of the results obtained in Grade 8, it lies 2.110 P.E. above the fourth grade median; on the basis of these five determinations, question 1 is given a value of −0.400 P.E.; that is, it lies .400 P.E. below the fourth grade median.

The last two figures in these tables (47 to 53) are not significant. They are included in order to make the weighted averages more

TABLE 45

DISTANCES OF EACH GRADE MEDIAN ABOVE EACH LOWER GRADE MEDIAN
AND ABOVE THE FOURTH GRADE MEDIAN IN TERMS OF P.E.

	Information Scales A and B		Thought Scales A and B	
	Distance Above Next Lower Grade Median	Distance Above Fourth Grade Median	Distance Above Next Lower Grade Median	Distance Above Fourth Grade Median
Grade 5	2.284	2.284	1.923	1.923
Grade 6	1.407	3.691	1.836	3.759
Grade 7	0.494	4.185	0.946	4.705
Grade 8	1.107	5.292	1.139	5.844

	Character Scales A and B		Character Scale L	
	Distance Above Next Lower Grade Median	Distance Above Fourth Grade Median	Distance Above Next Lower Grade Median	Distance Above Fourth Grade Median
Grade 5	1.545	1.545	1.185	1.185
Grade 6	1.174	2.719	1.099	2.284
Grade 7	0.962	3.681	0.592	2.876
Grade 8	0.681	4.362	0.765	3.641

precise, and especially in order to facilitate any work that may be done in extending these scales.

Tables 47 to 53 are constructed by adding to the P.E. distance of each question or problem above or below its own grade median the distance its own grade median is above the fourth grade median. In Grade 5, in Table 44, question 1 lies 2.958 P.E. below its own grade median. The median of Grade 5 is 2.284 P.E. above the median of Grade 4. Hence adding to −2.958 P.E. the +2.284 P.E. we obtain −0.674 P.E., the location of question 1 with reference to the fourth grade median as given under Grade 5 in Table 47. In Grade 6, in Table 44, question 1 lies 2.667 P.E. below its own grade median. The median of Grade 6 is 3.691 P.E. above the median of Grade 4. Hence adding to −2.667 P.E. the +3.691 we obtain +1.024 P.E., the location of question 1 with reference to the fourth grade median as given under Grade 6 in Table 47.

In Table 45 are given the P.E. distances of each grade median above the fourth grade median. These are derived or taken directly from Tables 33 to 36.

To determine the P.E. values assigned to each question in the last columns of Tables 47 to 53 a weighted average of the five determinations is taken. Inasmuch as the few dull pupils who have been promoted into the upper grades unduly increase the P.E. distances of the easy questions above the fourth grade median, the following system of weighting has been adopted. The determinations by the grade distribution whose median is **not**

TABLE 47

THE POSITION OF EACH QUESTION IN EACH GRADE AND ITS AVERAGE POSITION WHEN IT IS REFERRED TO THE FOURTH GRADE MEDIAN AS A POINT OF REFERENCE

Information A

	Grade 4	Grade 5	Grade 6	Grade 7	Grade 8	Weighted Average
1	−1.622	−0.674	+1.024	+0.968	+2.110	−0.400
2	−1.374	+0.322	+0.945	+1.418	+2.181	+0.155
3	−1.110	+0.258	+1.729	+2.197	+3.058	+1.396
4	+0.145	+1.904	+2.122	+2.493	+2.695	+1.607
5	−0.004	+1.129	+1.800	+3.045	+4.497	+2.125
6	+1.549	+2.859	+3.376	+2.782	+3.199	+2.798
7	+0.702	+0.933	+2.378	+2.529	+3.357	+1.829
8	+1.803	+2.706	+2.746	+3.272	+4.441	+3.314
9	+1.302	+2.381	+3.384	+3.520	+4.392	+3.143
10	+1.979	+3.053	+4.021	+4.081	+4.652	+3.694
11	+3.077	+4.103	+3.591	+4.330	+4.668	+4.150
12	+1.438	+2.284	+4.175	+4.420	+5.050	+3.650
13	+3.450	+4.319	+2.973	+4.603	+4.660	+4.081
14	+3.111	+2.731	+4.279	+4.592	+5.318	+4.202
15	+3.571	+4.135	+4.477	+4.941	+5.538	+4.809
16	+1.391	+2.944	+3.448	+4.958	+3.774	+3.440
17	+3.938	+2.210	+4.250	+4.712	+5.124	+4.070
18	[1]	+5.395	+6.253	+5.218	+5.649	+5.597
19	+2.257	+3.630	+4.918	+5.194	+5.847	+4.764
20	+3.938	+5.466	+6.377	+6.582	+7.254	+6.557
21	[1]	+6.104	+5.653	+5.594	+6.011	+5.812
22	[1]	+6.222	+5.015	+5.965	+6.378	+5.703
23	+4.275	+5.927	+5.996	+6.516	+6.638	+6.254
24	[1]	[1]	[1]	[1]	+7.838	+7.838
25	[1]	+5.927	+5.190	+5.996	+6.417	+5.870
26	+4.275	+5.584	+5.825	+6.299	+6.672	+6.161
27	[2]	[2]	+7.629	+7.531	+7.537	+7.554
28	[2]	[2]	+5.368	+5.286	+5.505	+5.407
29	-	-	+6.397	+6.625	+7.336	+6.785
30			+5.879	+6.529	+6.791	+6.497
33			+7.629	+8.460	+8.126	+8.093
34	[2]	[2]	[1]	[1]	+9.935	+9.935

[1] Indicates that no pupils in the grade answered the question correctly.
[2] Indicates that the question was not tried by the grade.

more than 1 P.E. from the location of the questions as given in Table 44 are assigned a value of 10; the determinations by the grade distribution whose median is more than 1 P.E. and less than 2 P.E. from the location of the questions are assigned a value of 6; the determinations by the grade distribution whose median is more than 2 P.E. and less than 3 P.E. from the location of the questions are assigned a value of 3; while the determinations by the grade distribution whose median is more than 3 P.E. from the location of the questions are assigned a value of 1. This system of weighting gives the greater values to the locations of questions which are nearer the medians of the grade distributions and at the same time gives to the locations of the

TABLE 48

THE POSITION OF EACH QUESTION IN EACH GRADE AND ITS AVERAGE POSITION WHEN IT IS REFERRED TO THE FOURTH GRADE MEDIAN AS A POINT OF REFERENCE

Information B

	Grade 4	Grade 5	Grade 6	Grade 7	Grade 8	Weighted Average
1	−2.370	−1.799	−0.034	+0.735	+1.209	−0.999
2	−1.926	+0.417	+0.676	+1.039	+2.181	−0.345
3	+0.464	+1.015	+2.918	+2.723	+3.749	+2.072
4	−0.156	+1.912	+2.541	+2.500	+1.354	+1.489
5	+0.689	+1.904	+2.259	+2.963	+3.313	+2.030
6	+1.033	+2.295	+2.305	+3.338	+3.550	+2.569
7	+0.547	+1.784	+3.246	+3.705	+4.485	+2.753
8	+0.807	+3.197	+2.667	+3.681	+3.848	+2.760
10	+3.346	+1.366	+3.202	+3.123	+4.142	+2.806
11	+2.746	+3.215	+2.122	+2.583	+2.881	+2.759
12	+3.346	+2.940	+4.503	+4.237	+5.124	+4.253
13	+3.111	+4.087	+4.343	+4.148	+4.301	+4.204
14	+4.275	+3.341	+4.729	+4.595	+5.031	+4.513
15	+1.196	+2.721	+3.388	+3.373	+3.860	+2.979
16	+2.357	+3.597	+4.315	+4.304	+5.034	+4.235
17	+3.111	+4.119	+4.631	+5.185	+5.764	+4.962
18	[1]	+6.222	+4.343	+4.237	+5.374	+4.702
19	+2.631	+4.541	+5.106	+4.712	+5.733	+4.863
20	[1]		+5.948	+5.381	+5.505	+5.535
21	[1]	+4.111	+5.635	+5.647	+6.036	+5.746
22	+2.597	+3.475	+4.654	+5.045	+6.023	+4.765
23	[1]	[1]	+6.339	+7.200	+8.126	+7.227
24	+4.083	+5.790	+5.948	+5.870	+6.427	+5.970
25	+3.725	+4.095	+4.673	+4.788	+5.273	+4.746
26	+4.600	+6.222	+5.135	+6.362	+6.393	+5.828
27	[2]	[2]	+5.972	+5.728	+5.784	+5.796
28	[2]	[2]	+5.411	+5.350	+5.377	+5.542
29	-	-	+5.228	+5.950	+6.297	+5.944
30			+7.086	+7.531	+6.948	+7.034
33			[1]	+8.460	+8.742	+8.601
34	-	-	+6.480	+6.931	+7.375	+6.928

questions that are farthest from the medians of the grade distributions some value.

Table 46 shows in detail the method of determining the weighted average for questions 1 and 4 of Table 47. ·

TABLE 46

METHOD OF DETERMINING THE WEIGHTED-AVERAGE VALUES OF THE TASKS

	Question 1	Question 4
Grade 4..............	6 x −1.622= −9.732	10 x +0.145= + 1.450
Grade 5..............	3 x −0.674= −2.022	10 x +1.904= +19.040
Grade 6..............	3 x +1.024= +3.072	6 x +2.122= +12.732
Grade 7..............	1 x +0.968= +0.968	6 x +2.493= +14.958
Grade 8..............	1 x +2.110= +2.110	3 x +2.695= + 8.085
Weighted Average....	−0.400	+ 1.607

Figs. 17 to 23 give the facts of the last columns of Tables 47 to 53 represented on a linear projection. These figures show the location in terms of P.E. of each question or problem with refer-

TABLE 49

Thought A

	Grade 4	Grade 5	Grade 6	Grade 7	Grade 8	Weighted Average
1	−0.190	+1.028	+2.814	+3.540	+4.116	+1.963
2	−0.484	+1.047	+2.463	+2.977	+3.780	+1.417
3	+0.689	+1.589	+3.200	+3.932	+4.591	+2.644
4	+0.940	+2.110	+3.471	+4.049	+4.971	+3.108
5a	+2.881	+3.287	+4.085	+4.537	+4.958	+4.209
5b	+2.514	+3.145	+3.356	+3.535	+4.382	+3.466
5c	+2.269	+2.658	+3.078	+3.199	+3.809	+2.962
6	[1]	+3.539	+3.659	+4.638	+5.159	+4.327
7	+1.602	+2.905	+4.096	+4.556	+5.434	+3.902
8	+3.820	+3.314	+4.058	+4.880	+5.364	+4.506
10a	[1]	+5.373	+6.664	+6.850	+7.119	+6.740
10b	+2.834	+3.411	+3.987	+4.593	+4.881	+3.932
10c	+4.275	+4.241	+4.860	+4.213	+5.348	+4.725
11a	+2.986	+3.332	+3.674	+4.142	+4.844	+3.988
11b	+4.083	+4.228	+4.541	+5.016	+5.703	+4.981
12	+1.749	+2.914	+3.919	+4.428	+4.825	+3.548
13	+2.834	+2.947	+4.096	+4.772	+5.325	+4.310
14	+3.077	+3.987	+3.543	+4.511	+5.522	+4.435
15a	+3.111	+4.204	+5.429	+5.050	+5.874	+5.251
15b	[1]	+5.142	+6.774	+5.636	+7.119	+6.166
16a	[2]	+2.792	+4.077	+4.475	+5.196	+4.135
16b		+4.111	+4.991	+5.027	+5.948	+5.242
17		+4.609	+5.361	+5.801	+6.686	+5.906
18		+3.608	+4.869	+5.587	+6.379	+5.328
19		+3.202	+4.584	+4.865	+5.777	+4.790
20a		+4.228	+5.375	+5.729	+6.427	+5.743
20b		+4.967	+5.562	+5.845	+6.407	+5.977
21		+3.219	+4.894	+5.065	+6.094	+5.008
22		+4.967	+5.914	+6.155	+6.312	+6.137

ence to the fourth grade median, which has been taken as an arbitrary point of reference. In Fig. 17, for instance, the distance that question 6 is above this arbitrary point of reference may be spoken of as being twice as far above the arbitrary point of reference as question 3, but question 6 cannot be called twice as difficult as question 3. Only the determination of the absolute zero point of history ability with respect to information would enable one to speak in such terms as one class possesses twice as much ability along information lines in history as another class.

An approximation to such an absolute zero could be obtained by extending the scales at their lower extremes down to questions or tasks so easy that experts would regard them as of almost zero difficulty. The method used in this study applied to such questions in the case of American children in Grades 4, 3, 2, and 1 would then supply the measures of the distances, in terms of the

TABLE 50

THE POSITION OF EACH QUESTION IN EACH GRADE AND ITS AVERAGE POSITION WHEN IT IS REFERRED TO THE FOURTH GRADE MEDIAN AS A POINT OF REFERENCE

Thought B

	Grade 4	Grade 5	Grade 6	Grade 7	Grade 8	Weighted Average
1	−0.727	+0.632	+1.514	+2.057	+2.680	+0.421
2a	+0.209	+0.467	+2.246	+2.787	+3.474	+1.468
2b	+0.492	+1.167	+2.846	+3.519	+4.569	+2.228
3a	+2.269	+4.016	+4.695	+4.850	+5.248	+4.632
3b	+2.411	+3.977	+4.017	+4.182	+4.394	+3.984
3c	+2.986	+4.006	+4.135	+4.287	+4.580	+4.146
4	+1.643	+2.234	+3.402	+4.012	+5.134	+3.427
5	+2.530	+3.202	+3.287	+4.310	+4.792	+3.757
6	+3.300	+4.180	+2.904	+3.796	+4.734	+3.708
7a	+2.986	+3.726	+4.507	+4.638	+4.643	+4.303
7b	+2.234	+2.637	+3.255	+3.677	+4.382	+3.256
8	+3.300	+3.073	+3.882	+4.675	+5.309	+4.335
9	+2.631	+3.274	+3.700	+4.216	+4.953	+4.005
10	+2.439	+3.202	+4.271	+5.146	+5.929	+4.615
11	+3.300	+4.485	+5.813	+5.591	+5.313	+5.304
12a	+2.726	+3.608	+4.314	+4.846	+5.224	+4.453
12b	+4.600	+4.180	+4.976	+5.150	+5.556	+5.135
13a	+2.986	+2.783	+3.755	+4.197	+4.668	+3.700
13b	+3.300	+3.532	+4.727	+5.158	+5.650	+4.860
14a	[1]	+5.743	+6.836	+7.116	+7.453	+7.149
14b	+3.146	+3.984	+4.628	+4.944	+4.922	+4.633
15	+2.631	+3.355	+4.351	+4.504	+5.096	+4.295
16	[2]	+4.780	+5.388	+6.261	+6.476	+5.959
17	[2]	+4.734	+5.240	+5.112	+5.646	+5.283
18	-	+4.855	+5.508	+6.321	+6.708	+6.104
19		+5.142	+6.040	+6.341	+6.305	+6.217
20a		+3.711	+4.064	+4.873	+5.372	+4.593
20b		+5.142	+6.198	+7.284	+7.507	+6.971
21		+5.181	+6.338	+6.759	+7.151	+6.721
22	•	+5.648	+6.664	+7.203	+7.968	+7.715

variability of a grade, of the zero-difficulty questions from the fourth grade median. Such questions might be: For the Information Scales—"In what country do you live?" "Is the United States the name of a nation or of an animal"? "Was George Washington an American or a Chinaman"? For the Thought Scales they might be—"The Indians built wigwams. Then they lived in the wigwams. Did they live in the wigwams before they built them?" "The Indians used skins in making their wigwams. They got the skins from animals. Did they have to kill the animals before they built their wigwams?" "A man built a house. Then he lived in it. Did he live in it before he built it?" For the Character Scales they might be— "A girl ate a peach. Then she said she did not eat it. She spent ten cents for candy. Then she said she did not spend it. She bit her sister. Then she said she did not bite her. Was the girl a liar?"

TABLE 51

THE POSITION OF EACH QUESTION IN EACH GRADE AND ITS AVERAGE POSITION WHEN IT IS REFERRED TO THE FOURTH GRADE MEDIAN AS A POINT OF REFERENCE

Character A

	Grade 4	Grade 5	Grade 6	Grade 7	Grade 8	Weighted Average
1	+0.620	+1.389	+2.123	+2.624	+3.348	+1.836
2	+0.693	+1.519	+2.030	+2.657	+2.947	+1.810
3	+0.612	+1.724	+2.547	+3.192	+3.823	+2.379
4	+1.884	+2.874	+3.145	+3.648	+3.831	+3.209
5	+0.847	+1.314	+1.569	+1.946	+4.559	+2.102
6a	+1.506	+2.517	+2.924	+3.502	+3.673	+2.939
6b	+1.357	+2.494	+2.778	+3.169	+3.467	+2.765
7a	+2.035	+2.550	+2.891	+3.220	+3.440	+2.997
7b	+1.835	+2.680	+3.270	+3.849	+4.104	+3.317
8	+1.677	+2.597	+2.962	+3.370	+3.706	+3.000
9	+1.269	+2.994	+3.211	+2.967	+3.055	+2.801
10	+1.444	+2.499	+3.351	+3.845	+4.047	+3.175
11	+2.746	+3.580	+3.946	+4.185	+4.362	+4.003
12	²	+3.619	+3.994	+4.293	+4.318	+4.170
13a	²	+3.471	+3.619	+3.935	+4.116	+3.820
13b	-	+3.814	+4.256	+4.621	+4.703	+4.490
14		+4.271	+4.288	+4.681	+4.593	+4.526
15a		+3.648	+4.021	+4.471	+4.941	+4.454
15b		+3.850	+4.282	+4.762	+4.815	+4.558

It would be necessary in the experiment, of course, to separate ignorance of facts from ignorance of language, and also inability to infer from inability to understand words. Possibly tests with pictures could be used to better advantage.

In default of such an experimental placing of the absolute zero for these three types of scales, which the author hopes to undertake later, the results of such *a priori* placings as may be made can be shown by a sample. Suppose, for instance, that the absolute zero for each scale be located provisionally at a point representing the probable ability of the lowest pupil in Grade 2 (−4.5 P.E. from the median of Grade 2). Assume also that the median for Grade 2 is as far below the median of Grade 4 as the median of Grade 4 is below that of Grade 6. This, of course, is purely a provisional arrangement, and would be used only when it is absolutely necessary to make some assumption about the absolute zero.

On the basis of these assumptions the values of Tables 47 and 48 would, when referred to the provisional absolute zero, be increased each by 2.284+1.407+4.5, or 8.191; and the hardest questions of the Information Scales would be counted as about 2½ times as "hard" as the easiest. The values of Tables 49 and 50 would be increased each by 1.923+1.836+4.5, or 8.259; and

TABLE 52

THE POSITION OF EACH QUESTION IN EACH GRADE AND ITS AVERAGE POSITION WHEN IT IS REFERRED TO THE FOURTH GRADE MEDIAN AS A POINT OF REFERENCE

Character B

	Grade 4	Grade 5	Grade 6	Grade 7	Grade 8	Weighted Average
1	+0.612	+1.181	+1.564	+2.059	+2.318	+1.332
2a	+1.859	+2.751	+3.122	+3.385	+3.639	+3.074
2b	+1.201	+2.201	+2.431	+2.754	+3.227	+2.391
3	+0.786	+2.057	+2.760	+3.525	+3.959	+2.617
4	+1.997	+2.670	+3.110	+3.528	+3.878	+3.170
5a	+1.563	+2.348	+3.022	+3.324	+3.685	+2.894
5b	+1.518	+2.013	+2.499	+2.886	+3.176	+2.432
6	+0.516	+1.056	+1.859	+2.352	+2.663	+1.533
7	+2.397	+3.364	+3.761	+4.130	+4.183	+3.802
8a	+1.670	+2.476	+3.509	+3.954	+4.284	+3.309
8b	+2.789	+3.790	+4.151	+4.252	+4.481	+4.124
8c	+1.827	+2.960	+3.930	+4.400	+4.545	+3.730
9	²	+2.436	+3.030	+3.581	+3.795	+3.210
10	²	+3.014	+3.451	+3.581	+3.831	+3.519
11	-	+4.193	+4.707	+5.096	+5.458	+4.958
12		+2.936	+3.859	+4.177	+4.749	+4.063
13a		+3.489	+4.355	+4.471	+5.123	+4.468
13b		+3.690	+4.645	+5.237	+5.824	+5.014
14		+4.622	+5.367	+5.903	+6.018	+5.733

TABLE 53

THE POSITION OF EACH QUESTION IN EACH GRADE AND ITS AVERAGE POSITION WHEN IT IS REFERRED TO THE FOURTH GRADE MEDIAN AS A POINT OF REFERENCE

Character L

	Grade 4	Grade 5	Grade 6	Grade 7	Grade 8	Weighted Average
1	+0.913	+1.465	+1.761	+1.990	+2.550	+1.665
2	+0.387	+1.174	+1.632	+2.038	+2.673	+1.580
3a	+1.616	+2.391	+3.024	+3.206	+3.634	+2.921
3b	+1.892	+2.266	+2.768	+3.092	+3.398	+2.798
4	+1.506	+2.476	+3.091	+3.313	+3.745	+2.985
5	+1.663	+2.660	+2.908	+3.175	+3.533	+2.907
6	+1.462	+2.295	+2.815	+2.857	+3.330	+2.680
7a	²	+2.350	+2.718	+2.917	+2.989	+2.787
7b	²	+3.430	+3.840	+4.077	+4.244	+4.009
8a	-	+2.761	+3.096	+3.317	+3.376	+3.179
8b		+3.299	+3.893	+4.145	+4.180	+3.997
9a		+3.120	+3.602	+3.710	+3.937	+3.650
9b		+3.036	+3.619	+3.957	+4.376	+3.765
10		+2.828	+3.322	+3.675	+4.017	+3.556

the hardest question of the Thought Scales would be about $1\frac{7}{8}$ times as "hard" as the easiest. Each of the values of Tables 51 and 52 would be raised by 1.545+1.174+4.5, or 7.219; and the hardest question of Character Scales A and B would be about $1\frac{1}{2}$ times as "hard" as the easiest.

Any investigator who needs to assume some absolute zero may conveniently define his assumption in the way just illustrated.

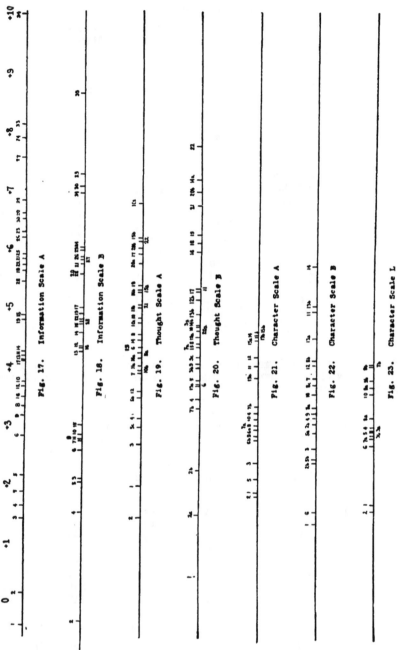

Fig. 17. Information Scale A

Fig. 18. Information Scale B

Fig. 19. Thought Scale A

Fig. 20. Thought Scale B

Fig. 21. Character Scale A

Fig. 22. Character Scale B

Fig. 23. Character Scale L

Figs. 17–23. Linear Projection of the Average Positions of Each Question

KEYS TO THE HISTORY SCALES

Answers to Questions of Information Scale A

QUESTION   CREDIT

1   3 = Indians (Indies in Grades 4 and 5); redskins, copper colored people.

     0 = Savages, natives.

2   8 = Washington, Grant, Lee, Schuyler, Sherman, Jackson, Warren, Greene.

     0 = Wolfe, Burgoyne, Admiral Dewey.

3   3 = Wigwam, teepee, long house, tent.

     0 = Caves, huts, tents and mounds, forests, camps, tents and canoes, in wigwams and log cabins, long houses and trees.

4   = Lincoln.

5   3 = Pilgrims, Plymouth, people of Plymouth, early settlers at Plymouth.

     0 = English, Americans, Indians, Puritans, Quakers, Christians.

6   3 = With Spain, Spain, Spanish; Spanish American War.

7   3 = Cabot, Vespucius, Sir Walter Raleigh, Drake, Champlain, De Soto, LaSalle, Balboa, Lief Ericson, Eric the Red, Henry Hudson, Pizarro, Coronado, Ponce de Leon, Marquette.

     0 = Americus or Amerigo, Magellan, Baltimore, Marco Polo, America.

8   3 = Declaration of Independence.

     0 = Signing of Declaration of Independence; Day of Independence, Declaration Day, Independence.

9   3 = Fighting and hunting; hunting and war; hunting, fishing and fighting; hunting and fishing; fishing and shooting; fish and shoot animals; fishing and trapping.

     0 = Fighting and fishing.

10   3 = 3–5–1–2–4.

     1 = One interchange.   (See note below, answer to question 25.)

11   3 = (a) Civil War.

     (b) Revolutionary War, or War of 1776; with England and colonies; or War for Independence.

     (c) War of 1812.

     1 = Any two of the three.

12   3 = Passage to the Pacific, Pacific ocean, water route across North America, northwest passage, strait, route to the west, a short or new way or route to India or Asia or China; short route, new route; northwest passage to India, passage to India; shortest passage to India; northern passage to India.

     0 = East Indies or India; trading post, fur trade, new land, route to West Indies, southern route to India.

13   3 = Jefferson.

14   3 = (a) Spain or Spanish.

     (b) England, Great Britain or English.

     (c) France or French.

     (d) Holland, Netherlands or Dutch.

     0 = Inclusion of Portugal, Germany, Italy, or Russia as one of the four.

15   3 = (a) Burgoyne.
           (b) Cornwallis.
16   3 = Civil War, or War of 1862, or War between the North and
           the South.
        0 = Monitor and Merrimac.
17   3 = Iroquois; Five Nations or Six Nations.
        0 = Algonquins, Powhatan, Iroquois and Sioux.
18   3 = (a) Telegraph.
           (b) Telephone.
           (c) Wireless.
        1 = Any two of the three, or three correct with inclusion of some-
           thing not strictly applicable.
19   3 = Working on farms, farming.
20   3 = (a) Stagecoach, stage, coach, wagon, or carriage.
           (b) Horseback, horse.
           (c) Sailboat, sailing.
        0 = Boat, ship or water in place of sailboat or sailing; Flatboat,
           barges, rowboat, ferry or canoe in place of sailboat or sailing;
           Canal boats pulled by horses or mules, steamboat, bicycle,
           caravans, prairie schooners.
21   3 = (a) Cumberland road, National road, public road, highways,
           roads to the west.
           (b) Erie Canal.
           (c) Panama Canal.
        1 = Any two of the three correct; two correct and subway.
        0 = Inclusion of something not applicable as steam engine or
           wireless.
22   3 = Cotton gin and steamboat.
        0 = Eli Whitney and Robert Fulton.
23   3 = How to keep the Southern states in the Union, to hold the
           Union together, preserve the Union, keeping of the Union,
           holding of the Union, what to do about the secession of the
           Southern states; secession, breaking up of the Union, disunion
           or not, break between North and South; whether the states
           were free to secede, should the states be let leave the Union,
           whether the states had a right to leave the Union or not, states
           rights, how to treat the seceded states, what to do with the
           South.
        0 = War, Civil War, war with Confederates, fight over slavery,
           putting down the Confederates, fight, to see after the Civil
           War, whether he should declare war or not, war or peace;
           slavery, slavery question, whether there should be slavery or
           not, war or peace; how to set the slaves free, how to save the
           Union and abolish slavery, he had to free the slaves, put the
           Union together, question of slavery, slavery problem and
           preserving the Union, for freedom, to stop slavery, whether to
           admit the Southern states to the Union or not, to fight for the
           Civil War.
24   3 = (a) Civil Service Commission.
           (b) Interstate Commerce Commission.
        1 = Civil Service Commission or Interstate Commerce Commis-
           sion with the other omitted.
25   3 = 6–2–5–3–7–1–4.
        2 = One interchange, or two interchanges or one two-place dis-
           placement.
        1 = One three or more place displacement or one two-place dis-
           placement and one interchange; or one double interchange as
           3–2–1–4–5–6–7, or three interchanges.
           NOTE.—The answer to this type of question may be easily
           and quickly scored as follows: Assume that a pupil's order is

5–2–4–3–7–1–6. By placing it below the correct order thus

6–2–5–3–7–1–4
5–2–4–3–7–1–6

1 in the pupil's order corresponds to 1 in the correct order, 2 corresponds to 2 in the correct order, 3 corresponds to 3 in the correct order, 4 corresponds to 5 in the correct order, 5 corresponds to 6 in the correct order, 6 corresponds to 4 in the correct order and 7 corresponds to 7 in the correct order.

By writing down in a new order the numbers of the correct order to which the numbers of the pupil's order correspond when the latter are taken in the order 1–2–3–4–5–6–7 we have 1–2–3–5–6–4–7. This is an illustration of what is meant by a two-place displacement, the 4 being two places out of order. This order would be the pupil's actual arrangement of the events if the events themselves were arranged in the or er in which they occurred instead of being arranged by chance.

1–*3*–*2*–4–5–6–7 is an illustration of what is meant by one interchange, 1–*3*–*2*–*5*–*4*–*7*–*6* is an illustration of what is meant by three interchanges, 1–*4*–*3*–*2*–5–6–7 is an illustration of what is meant by a double interchange.

26   3 = 7–6–1–5–4–3–2.

2 = One interchange, or two interchanges or one two-place displacement.

1 = One three or more place displacement or one two-place displacement and one interchange; or one double interchange as 3–2–1–4–5–6–7, or three interchanges.

27   3 = 12 correct.

2 = 10 or 11 correct.

1 = 8 or 9 correct.

a = Morse.	*b* = Bell.	*c* = Cyrus Field.
d = Jefferson Davis.	*e* = Thomas Jefferson.	*f* = Hamilton.
g = Robert Morris.	*h* = Perry.	*i* = Henry Clay.
j = John Jay.	*k* = Edwin M. Stanton.	*l* = Roger B. Tany

28   3 = 7 correct.

2 = 6 correct.

1 = 5 correct.

> Morgan.
> Farragut.
> Dewey.
> Taylor.
> Thomas.
> Grant.
> Perry.

29   3 = 2–5–1–7–6–4–3.

2 = One interchange or two interchanges or one two-place displacement.

1 = One three or more place displacement; one two-place displacement and one interchange, or one double interchange as 3–2–1–4–5–6–7, or three interchanges.

30   3 = (*a*) Protection of slavery in the territories.

(*b*) The "gag rule" or suppression of abolition petitions in Congress.

(*c*) Annexation of Texas.

1 = The above three and one other one checked or any two of the above three and no others checked.

33   3 = Colonization and interference with South American republics. Establishing monarchies and recapture of Spain's colonies. Shouldn't settle in America—keep hands off all colonies that did not belong to them.

Russia planting colonies on the Pacific—Spain trying to regain her colonies.

0 = No more colonies to be planted—settlement by European nations, no colonies and Holy Alliance; Holy Alliance or extension of Holy Alliance system; to keep the Holy Alliance from helping Spain take back her colonies; no European country could get land in America.

34   3 = 7 correct.
      2 = 6 correct.
      1 = 5 correct.
            Polk.
            McKinley.
            Monroe.
            Cleveland.
            Roosevelt.
            Arthur or Garfield.
            Jackson.

NOTE:—To find the number of questions correctly answered by a pupil divide the total of his credits by 3.

ANSWERS TO QUESTIONS OF INFORMATION SCALE B

1   3 = Henry Hudson, Hendrick Hudson, H. Hudson, Hudson.
2   3 = George Washington, Washington.
3   3 = Cruelly, harshly, badly, roughly, unjustly, mean, wicked, barbarously, poorly; hostile, bad, cruel; abused them; fought hard against them; made slaves of them, like slaves, killed and conquered, cheated them, robbed them.
      0 = Kindly, very good, hated them; killed them, nice.
4   3 = Grant, Lee, Pickett, Johnson, Hood, McClellan, Thomas, Sheridan, Hooker, Pope.
5   3 = France.
6   3 = Lexington, Yorktown, Bunker Hill, Brandywine, White Plains, Saratoga, Princeton, Ft. Moultrie, Camden.
      0 = Burgoyne's defeat, Brandytown.
7   3 = Any two of these: bow and arrow; club; spear; tomahawk or hatchet, or ax.
      1 = Any one of the above and knives.
      0 = Bow and arrow; tomahawk, hatchet; bone crusher, stone hammer, sword, daggers.
8   3 = England, Great Britain, English, British.
10   3 = Cartier, Champlain, La Salle, Marquette, Joliet.
      0 = De Soto, Ponce de Leon.
11   3 = Any two of these: Philippines, Gadsden, Louisiana, Florida, Alaska.
      0 = Hawaii, Oregon, Texas, Northwest territory.
12   3 = Spain, France.
13   3 = (a) Exploring.
         (b) Settling.
         (c) Nation-making.
14   3 = (a) Holland—Dutch.
         (b) England—English.
         (c) France—French.
         (d) England—English.
      1 = Any three of the four correct.
      0 = Inclusion of Quakers or Pilgrims among the three.
15   3 = (a) Stagecoach, coach.
         (b) Railroad, locomotive.
16   3 = 3–5–1–4–2.

1 = One interchange. (See note below answer to 25 in Key to Information Questions Scale A.)

17   3 = Any three of these: Washington, Lee, Greene, Putnam, Gates, Stark, Marion, Schuyler, Warren, Sullivan, Herkimer.

1 = Any two of the above for the first two, with the third omitted or wrong.

0 = Any two of them with the first or second wrong, or including Lee or Lincoln.
Robert E. Lee, Clarke, Gage, Howe, Clinton, Jones, Wolfe, Lafayette.

18   3 = Reaper, harvester, machine for cutting grain, reaping machine.
0 = Iron plow and reaper, reaper and locomotive.

19   3 = Steam or steam engine.
0 = Water power and steam, water power, steamboat, railroad.

20   3 = (a) Cotton gin.
(b) Sewing machine or Howe's machine.

21   3 = (a) Catholics.
(b) Puritans.
(c) Quakers.
1 = Catholics, Puritans and Protestants; or Catholics, Protestants and Quakers.
Two out of the three correct, the other one being wrong or omitted.

22   3 = Canoes . . . . . . walking, running, on foot, trails, or small paths,
Paddling, rowing . . . . . . walking.
0 = Boat or water . . . . . . walking.
Horse, horseback, or riding . . . . . . walking, running or canoe.
Canoe, walking . . . . . . snowshoes.

23   3 = Protective tariff; tariff, high or low tariff.

24   3 = (a) Steamboat.
(b) Railroad, locomotive, or steam engine.
(c) Trolley car or automobile.
1 = Any two of the three correct, the other one being wrong or omitted.

25   3 = 2-7-1-6-3-5-4.
2 = One interchange or two interchanges or one two-place displacement.
1 = One three or more place displacement or one two-place displacement and one interchange, or one double interchange as 3-2-1-4-5-6-7 or three interchanges.
(See note below answer to 25 in Answers to Questions of Information Scale A.)

26   3 = 6-3-1-7-5-2-4.
2 = One interchange or two interchanges or one two-place displacement.
1 = One three or more place displacement or one two-place displacement and one interchange, or one double interchange as 3-2-1-4-5-6-7 or three interchanges.

27   3 = 12 correct.
2 = 10 or 11 correct.
1 = 8 or 9 correct.

Supreme Court judge	statesman
general	Supreme Court judge
inventor	statesman
preacher	inventor
president	general
inventor	president

28   3 = 7 correct.
2 = 6 correct.
1 = 5 correct.

0 = 4 correct.
　Revolutionary.
　Civil.
　Spanish-American.
　Mexican, 1845-8.
　Civil.
　Civil.
　1812.

29　3 = John Adams.
　Alexander Hamilton.
　Benjamin Franklin.
　Abraham Lincoln.
　George Washington.
　Daniel Webster.
　1 = One of these not checked in addition to the other three not checked.
　One besides these checked.

30　3 = 16 correct.
　2 = 14 or 15 correct.
　1 = 12 or 13 correct.

Missouri.	Henry Clay.
Kansas-Nebraska Act.	Stephen A. Douglas.
South Carolina.	John C. Calhoun.
Secession.	Jefferson Davis.
Monroe Doctrine.	Grover Cleveland.
Ordinance of 1787.	George Rogers Clark.
Black people not citizens.	Roger B. Taney.
War with Mexico.	James K. Polk.

33　3 = Extension of slavery in the territories, slavery in the territories, spread of slavery, slavery increasing.
　1 = Slavery movement.
　0 = Slavery, withdrawal of the Missouri Compromise, secession, doing away with slavery, abolition of slavery.

34　3 = (a) Protective tariff question.
　(b) Demand for a shorter working day.
　(c) Maintaining neutrality.
　(d) Extension of suffrage to another group of people.
　1 = One besides the above checked.
　One of these four unchecked, the rest also being unchecked.
　0 = Two of these four unchecked, the rest also being unchecked.

NOTE.—To find the number of questions correctly answered by a pupil divide the total of his credits by 3.

ANSWERS TO QUESTIONS OF THOUGHT SCALE A

QUESTION CREDIT

1　3 = In sailboats, by the wind.
　0 = In steamboats, in row boats, in row boats and logs, rafts, canoes, in wooden boats, boats, in flat boats, vessels, big ships, wooden boats.

2　3 = A short route to India, India; western passage to India, western route to India, northwest passage to India; a new way to India, a way to India, an easy way to India.
　2 = Indies or East Indies.
　0 = Asia, a passage to the west.

3　3 = 100 years ago there were no railroads, no trains or steamships, traveled by stagecoach or horses.
　(Today we have railroads.)

2 = Hard to travel, poor means of transportation; swift railroads now. (Traveling was so slow.)

1 = Did not have fast trains. (More mail carriers and railroads; quicker boats and trains, no railroads and telegraph.)

0 = They had no steam; no means of transportation, no means of traveling; they had sailboats then.

4
3 = The Northmen; Vikings, Lief Ericson.
0 = Columbus, Indians.

5a
3 = Make it cheaper; cheaper, lessen the cost, reduce the cost, got low, would become cheap; it would be cheap, cheap; (made cotton cheaper; made it more profitable.)
1 = 50 times cheaper.

5b
3 = Increase the amount, more cotton raised, more could be raised, large amount, huge quantities.
1 = 50 times as much or 100 times as much.

5c
3 = Lower the price, make it cheaper, make it cost less, go low, go down, cheaper; much cheaper, less, lower, make it very cheap, cheap cotton g   s, cheap.

6
3 = Sell it to the United States (or to America); sold it to the United States.
1 = (Sell it.)
0 = (To give it to the United States.)

7
3 = New inventions, invention of machinery, use of machinery. (They had machines, had no machines to raise it.)
2 = By an invention; invention of some specific machine, i. e., reaper; machinery. (Better machinery.)
1 = (Had different machinery or different tools, more machines, factories and mines; mining and making tools.)

8
3 = Manufacturing and mining (mining and factories, mining and smelting.)
1 = Manufacturing (or foundry work), (manufacturing of iron and manufacturing of cotton), mining.
0 = Iron work, coal (manufacturing and farming, mining and commerce, manufacturing and shipbuilding; mining and railroads).

10a
3 = There was not much under cultivation, very little cultivated, very small, not much was cultivated, very little, only a part, small parts; large amount of woodland.
0 = A great deal was cultivated, large proportion, large, it was immense, more than half; people did not have much land; people had large farms, large pieces of land.

10b
3 = Cheap, not expensive, very cheap, cost very little, price very low.
0 = Dear, expensive, not very cheap; cost nothing.

10c
3 = Did not know much about agriculture, very little knowledge, very limited; knew very little about fertilizing; very little knowledge about agriculture, poor farmers, very poor; very little, small.
1 = Did not know anything about agriculture, bad knowledge, very ignorant, bad; little agriculture.
0 = Very good, plenty of knowledge of farming; good; knew a great deal about agriculture; knew much about fertilizing.

11a
3 = Manufacturing of cotton goods, textile manufacturing, making clothing; manufacturing of cotton, cotton manufacturing.
2 = Manufacturing.
0 = Importation or exportation of cotton; commerce, cotton, cotton goods, making suits.

(For the values assigned to the answers in parentheses the author alone is responsible.)

11b   3 = It would stop it, it would stop cotton manufacturing; prevent England from getting the cotton, have no cotton to manufacture, cotton could not be sent to England. (Manufacturing in England would be almost stopped.)

            1 = Not as important, hurt the occupation; not good, very poor, bad r England; throw lots of workers out, put people out of work⚹o

            0 = England could not sell cotton or manufactured goods; stop its exportation, could not export it, could not send it out; stop England's trade with the South.

12   3 = Use of electricity or electric power; invention of electricity or electric power, electric power; electricity.

13   3 = To make money, to enrich their merchants, to grow rich, to gain, to make on the colonies, to get much out of their colonies; betterment of England.

            To gain trade, to gain control of the trade of the colonies; England wanted all the trade herself, to receive all our products and fix prices; to get Americans to send them their products.

            2 = So the colonies would not sell their goods to other countries for more money, not to trade with other countries, colonists might get things from other countries, so they would be the only country to get the benefit of their things; so she could get the best; to make her commerce big.

            To have full control over her colonies, to keep them from gaining their independence, to prevent the colonies from becoming too wealthy, to make the colonies less rich. So they could buy cheaper, to make the colonies pay more, to fix prices on colonial goods.

            1 = To tax the colonies, to get the tariff, to get more money, to pay the war debt.

            To keep the colonies small and weak, to gain a greater foothold, to oppress them.

            To get all the trade from Holland; wanted England to become mistress of the seas.

14   3 = Blockade the Southern ports, cut off the Southern trade with England, stop cotton trade, prevent the South from exporting cotton, prevent the South from selling cotton.

            0 = Stop manufactured articles going to the South; build factories, manufacture cotton goods, manufacture more things; to get possession of the South.

            (Blockade the ports and free the slaves.)

15a   3 = Royalists, the king's favorites, people who believed in the king; those who belonged to the Church of England; Cavaliers.

            2 = (High class people, rich people.)

15b   3 = Virginia (to the Southern colony).

16a   3 = Knew nothing about iron, did not know about iron, did not know how to use iron, did not know the use of iron.

            2 = Knew little about iron, did not know much about iron, did not use much iron, very rare, very poor knowledge, it was no good; did not know the value of iron.

16b   3 = Inefficient, considered poor now, not very good, very poor, not strong; crude, clumsy, hard to use.

            0 = They did not have many, had only a few tools; efficient, served their purpose all right, well-made, very useful, good, sharp, tried to do the best they could.

17   3 = Immigration from Ireland increased on account of the famine and declined when it ceased, Irish came over to escape the famine, famine caused immigration to increase; more Irish came to America when there was a famine in Ireland, number increased at the time of the famine.

2 = More food in the United States; came where there was no famine. (When conditions were bad in Ireland they came to America.)

1 = After the famine they did not come.

0 = The famine was over in 1851 or 1852; after the famine they came to America; too many people in Ireland. (All the Irish people came here during the famine.)

18   3 = Capturing British merchant vessels, attacking British merchant vessels (turned pirates, capture or attack them).

1 = Stop the trading, destroy the British vessels.

0 = Attack the British navy, build a navy.

19   3 = Made it by hand; women wove it; by spinning, using the loom, weaving the cotton; women made it, made it themselves.

2 = Smuggle it in from England or other countries, running the blockade.

1 = Made their own clothes, made clothing by hand; slaves made clothing.

0 = Trading with South American countries or other nations; obtained it from South America; got it from Europe, sent it to England to be made, build factories; got it from the North.

20a   3 = Yes: Because they did not have to pay a large tax; because it cost them nothing; their children would be educated free.

2 = Yes: Their children would become educated, their children would learn more and it would be cheaper.

1 = Yes: Children would not learn at home, children in rural communities had better opportunities; wanted as many children as possible to attend school, wanted their children to become educated; wanted to educate their children (they wanted a free education), could not afford to educate their children, workingmen were poor, had to pay to have their children educated.

20b   3 = No: It would raise the taxes on their farms, the tax was so high, could not afford to pay the tax; cost too much.

2 = No: Children could learn the necessary things at home, children did not have to go to school; taught their own children.

1 = No: Children needed in the home or on the farms; could afford to educate their children.

21   3 = Their own religious freedom, a religion for themselves, their own kind of religion, religious freedom for themselves, for their religion only, Puritan religion; all should have the same religion, to get every one to worship as they did, to have one religion.

2 = To worship as they pleased, as they saw fit, to believe as they wanted to, to go to a church of their own, to pray in their own way; tyrannical religious freedom, compel people to come to church or be punished.

1 = To run things their own way, government would have no say over them, to do what they wanted to do.

0 = Did not want to belong to the Church of England, free from Church of England, separate from the church; to purify the church; Presbyterians, simpler form of worship; true religious freedom; absolute religious freedom, free religious freedom, strict religious freedom; to make money; church attendance and Sabbath observance, to be a Christian and have liberty, Baptist, Catholic. (To belong to any church they wanted to.)

22   3 = They were Tories or loyalists; refused their aid to the colonies; favored the king, with the king, took the part of England, they had aided England against the colonists; they had fought against the revolutionists. (They were English; they went against the United States.)

1 = Traitors.
0 = They were in debt, government needed money; did not have a
strong government, very cruel and mean. (They did not
fight for America.)

NOTE.—To find the number of questions correctly answered by a pupil,
divide the total of his credits by 3.

ANSWERS TO QUESTIONS OF THOUGHT SCALE B

QUESTION   CREDIT

1   3 = United States ought to help France, help them, help them with
men and ships; to become an ally of France, to fight with them,
to go on the French side; to go to war with England.
1 = United States ought to go to war, fight.
0 = To interfere, to stop the war.

2a   3 = Answer indicating refusal; "No," "it was theirs."
1 = Fight, war.

2b   3 = Send an army to take it, attack the fort, fight for the fort,
attack the French, to have war (fight).
2 = Declare war, say they would fight; prepare for war, build a
fort and fight; capture the fort, take it.
0 = Chase them.

3a   3 = Increase it, more freight, more transportation, more extensive
trade.
0 = Carry a great deal; cheaper, less freight, decrease it.

3b   3 = Increase the value, raise the value, make it higher, dearer,
more expensive, make it valuable, make it expensive, expensive,
big value, would be valuable.
1 = Good effect.
0 = Decrease the value, make the land cheaper, valuable for factories; new cities along the canal; people settled along the
canal.

3c   3 = Increase the settlement, help build up the West, West would
become more settled; more people went to the West, increased
population; settled more quickly; opened up the West, West
would become settled, West would become great, settlers would
begin to go West (settled more thickly).
2 = More people travelled to the West; more people went by the
canal; travelling made easier; quicker to go to the West.

4   3 = Food was scarce, lack of food, there was no food in that time,
starvation, the people had nothing to eat, there was not enough
food.
2 = Hardships of the Jamestown colony, bad times, misery, suf-
fering. (They needed help.)
1 = Hunger, p vert . (They were hungry, they were poor.)
0 = Settlers did not cultivate the land, lazy and did not want to
work, careless; a government was needed; were not able to
support themselves.

5   3 = Monmouth, Lundy's Lane, Petersburg.
6   3 = Increased it (made it more profitable).
7a   3 = Increased, more money was invested in manufacturing, more,
greater, more people invested, a large amount was invested,
a lot of money was spent in manufacturing.
1 = More factories were built, more factories; more things were
manufactured, more manufacturing was done, manufacturing
increased, much manufacturing done.
0 = More than one-half invested.

7b   3 = More goods manufactured, increased, more.
2 = More manufacturing, more factories, a lot of goods were manufactured, large.

0 = One-half amount of goods, more than one-half, one-half.

8   3 = Manufacturing, making our own goods.

0 = In cotton; commerce, agriculture, mining.

9   3 = Immigration was rapidly increasing, increase of immigration, immigration rapidly increased, more people came over.

2 = More came to America every year; population was increasing, United States was growing, growth, immigration steadily increased.

1 = Much immigration, many people came to the United States, one of the causes of the growth of America, growth of cities.

10   3 = Massachusetts.

11   3 = Right to vote, suffrage, the ballot, to choose their rulers.

0 = Right to hold office, a law passed.

12a   3 = In the factories, in manufacturing places.

2 = They were working. (In some manufacturing state or city.)

0 = In shops; at home or working on the farms; in the fields; no more children born.

12b   3 = Compulsory education, children must go to school until a certain age; child labor laws, child labor is forbidden, law forbidding children under fourteen to work; they must have a certain age, cannot work under sixteen, have to have working papers.

2 = Against the laws, kept under a certain law, prevented by laws, not allowed because of the law, there are rules which are enforced.

0 = Because there are enough workmen, lack of money, child labor is reduced, in hospital, in their graves, children would have been found dead, teachers are not as mean as they were in those days. (Board of Education would not let them, forced to go to school.)

13a   3 = Shipbuilding.

1 = Lumbering.

0 = Commerce, transportation, carpentering.

13b   3 = Injured, lessened, decreased or damaged it, destroyed, stopped, killed, spoiled, ruined, bad effect, could not send them out.

0 = Stopped trading; ships could not go out.

14a   3 = Very little, not much, was not large.

0 = Increasing rapidly; schools began to increase, it became larger, it was extending rapidly; it extended very much, there was a steady increase, it increased; it had spread greatly; greatly increased, was increased; increase.

14b   3 = Wanted it; believed in it; valued it, thought it important, thought it good, favorable, greatly favorable, favored it, friendly, very good, liked it; were pleased with it, showed great respect toward public education; interested in public education; they were anxious to have an education, wanted to be educated, wanted an education.

0 = Liberal education.

15   3 = They would decrease, become smaller, diminish, make them small, smaller.

2 = They would be small, they were small, they were not large, small, very small.

0 = Too big.

16   3 = (a) Connecticut, (b) Virginia, (b) Pennsylvania, (b) New York, (a) Rhode Island.

17   3 = Because the first census was taken in 1790, we take the census now and then we didn't, there was no census taken; because the census was taken in 1790, but not in 1650.

2 = The census was taken in 1790; the census was taken, we were counted in 1790.

0 = Census is taken every ten years, because we were not a country until 1789.

18   3 = More foreigners in the Northern cities, live in the Northern cities or come to the Northern cities; Northern states or North have more people of foreign birth; Southern states or South have not as many foreigners; foreigners settled in the North.

2 = Many foreign people in the Northern cities, Southern cities had few foreigners.

1 = All foreigners went to the manufacturing states of the North.

0 = Population of North larger than that of the South or vice-versa; Northern cities were settled by foreigners.

19   3 = A too strong central government; national supremacy, nation has too much power; not having state rights, that they would not have any state rights, their power would be taken away.

2 = Congress having too much power; powers were given to Congress by the Constitution; Congress has the power to do every thing.

1 = Of Congress.

0 = A monarchy (of the Constitution).

20a   3 = No cable; no direct means of communication, no means of communication except by boat, no quick means of communication, took long to spread the news, because it took so long for the news to cross the ocean, no easy way to send a message, no means of quick transportation, had to come in sailing ships; no wireless.

2 = No telegraph, no ocean steamers, no fast ocean steamers, slow vessels.

1 = Slow traveling.

0 = Bad communication, did not have good transportation; delayed, few ships, no railroads; had to travel under water, English kept it back, on account of the weather, mail traveled slowly; no postmen, had no good roads; all American and British ships were lost; (telephone not invented).

20b   3 = No effect, nothing.

0 = Change them in favor of the American side, gave more to America, more benefit to the Americans; we could make larger demands; Americans could demand more.
Peace would be restored quicker; quicken arrangements. Delay peace, take long; it would be prolonged; treaty would be no good; have to make another, bust them up, there would be no peace, change the treaty, bad effect, Americans would be victorious.

21   3 = Dutch settlement was becoming stronger, more Dutch had come to America, New Amsterdam settled in 1623.

1 = Dutch had been preparing, had been raising an army, had been building a navy.

0 = English were trying to get New Netherlands.

22   3 = There were not railways to ship it around, no means of transportation; not many railroads or ways to carry it.

1 = Too expensive to ship it around, it was too costly; water power was cheaper than coal (poor means of transportation, could not transport it quickly enough).

0 = People had water power; did not have the machinery to use it; there was not enough, not found everywhere; water power better, did not know its usefulness, did not need it, because they could not get fuel, could not get it everywhere.

NOTE.—To find the number of questions correctly answered by a pupil, divide the total of his credits by 3.

Answers to Questions of Character Scale A

1	indifferent	cowardly	cautious	polite	*brave*
	courageous	spiteful	fearful	*daring*	timid
2	cowardly	prudent	ignoble	*fearless*	*daring*
	treacherous	cautious	*courageous*	selfish	faithless
3	*just*	obstinate	irresolute	servile	resentful
	compliant	*honorable*	*patriotic*	unfair	submissive
4	ignoble	meddlesome	*courageous*	reckless	foolhardy
	crabbed	*persistent*	spiteful	*undaunted*	peevish
5	cruel	timid	cowardly	mean	*self-sacrificing*
	crafty	*heroic*	selfish	*noble*	treacherous
6a	faithful	*false*	honest	*unscrupulous*	fearless
	dishonest	resolute	gentle	revengeful	spiteful
6b	timid	selfish	*honest*	unscrupulous	*fearless*
	cowardly	spiteful	*resolute*	revengeful	dishonest
7a	frightened	*resolute*	excited	terrified	careless
	deliberate	wavering	timid	cowardly	*cool*
7b	treacherous	brave	crafty	*excited*	cool
	terrified	courageous	resolute	bold	*irresolute*
8	cautious	tactful	*callous*	generous	courteous
	thoughtful	sympathetic	*rude*	*insolent*	considerate
9	heroic	*treacherous*	defiant	noble	*deceitful*
	brave	*untrustworthy*	honest	daring	timid
10	humane	disloyal	merciful	*cruel*	heroic
	careless	kind	*crafty*	noble	*stealthy*
11	*intrepid*	dismayed	gentle	shrinking	*resolute*
	cowardly	treacherous	timid	*dauntless*	deceitful
12	kind	bitter	*sarcastic*	generous	cautious
	humorous	ignoble	abusive	sympathetic	*ready-witted*
13a	*negligent*	courageous	zealous	*rash*	intrepid
	ardent	*shortsighted*	capable	firm	undaunted
13b	wary	selfish	cautious	cowardly	*incautious*
	negligent	prudent	zealous	*incompetent*	defiant
14	tolerant	*bigoted*	fair	generous	*narrow-minded*
	open-minded	daring	*prejudiced*	liberal	deceitful
15a	tactful	petty	noble	*daring*	*impudent*
	generous	honorable	cowardly	*amusing*	courteous
15b	prudent	tactful	*impulsive*	just	deliberate
	modest	*resentful*	cool	generous	*touchy*

NOTE.—Three credits are given for each problem in which the three words are correctly underlined or the three motives correctly checked. One credit is given for each problem in which two out of the three words are correctly underlined or two out of the three motives are correctly checked. One credit is also given in case the three words are correctly underlined and also one wrong word is underlined; and likewise when the three motives are correctly checked and one wrong motive is also checked. To find the number of problems correctly done by a pupil divide the total of his credits by 3. Correct answers are printed in italics.

Answers to Questions of Character Scale B

1	careless	cruel	timid	*courageous*	cautious
	foolish	*heroic*	*noble*	selfish	spiteful
2a	careless	*enduring*	disloyal	*steadfast*	faint-hearted
	wavering	seditious	*persevering*	treacherous	ignoble
2b	cowardly	deceitful	reckless	*self-sacrificing*	timid
	faint-hearted	callous	*faithful*	unfeeling	*courageous*
3	defiant	*honorable*	*brave*	false	cowardly
	servile	irresolute	unfair	*gallant*	stupid

4	shiftless	careless	*enduring*	foolhardy	cowardly
	timid	*dauntless*	lazy	*stout-hearted*	negligent
5a	treacherous	*fearless*	resentful	cowardly	deceitful
	independent	selfish	*resolute*	submissive	crafty
5b	prudent	*faithless*	dependable	just	*false*
	upright	conscientious	loyal	*untrustworthy*	independent
6	selfish	treacherous	*daring*	cruel	spiteful
	timid	fearful	*brave*	*bold*	cowardly
7	weak	timid	incapable	*sympathetic*	incompetent
	cowardly	negligent	*tactful*	*chivalrous*	dishonest
8a	spiteful	petty	*independent*	ignoble	*daring*
	reckless	wavering	foolhardy	*patriotic*	timid
8b	brave	patriotic	*unjust*	courageous	prudent
	contemptible	just	judicious	*despicable*	careless
8c	unfair	*just*	timid	traitorous	*free*
	despicable	submissive	cautious	*independent*	ignoble
9	rude	spiteful	blunt	*clever*	tactless
	shrewd	abusive	unfair	*humorous*	discourteous
10	noble	*rude*	heroic	*tactless*	courteous
	gallant	*discourteous*	considerate	tactful	courageous
11	cowardly	bold	*considerate*	*judicious*	weak
	yielding	daring	dilatory	*prudent*	timid
12	self-seeking	*patriotic*	servile	defiant	*independent*
	ignoble	insolent	stubborn	*democratic*	obstinate
13a	cowardly	servile	obstinate	*firm*	stubborn
	compliant	*honorable*	submissive	*conscientious*	irresolute
13b	*shrewd*	unjust	suspicious	credulous	*clever*
	servile	*sagacious*	false	deceitful	treacherous
14	just	*simple*	fair	careful	*incompetent*
	wary	frank	honest	*credulous*	watchful

NOTE.—For computation of scores see note on answers to Character Scale A, page 63.

ANSWERS TO QUESTIONS OF CHARACTER SCALE L

1. She may have felt that they would probably all be killed and that she would rather die fighting as the men did.
    She may have felt that it was her plain duty.
    She may have felt that it was worth risking her life to save those in the fort.
2. He may have done it because he thought so much of his boy.
    He may have felt that it was his duty.
    He may have feared that he could never be happy again if his little son were killed.
3a. They may have thought that the white soldiers had the advantage.
    They may have been too frightened to oppose the white soldiers.
    They may have wanted to save their own lives at any cost.
3b. They may have wanted to make the Indians fear and dread them.
    They may have wanted to defeat the Indians completely.
    They may have felt that this was too good an opportunity of punishing the Indians for past ravages to lose.
4. They may have wanted to take revenge on the white men for having injured some one of their kin.
    They may have been in a rage over some act which they thought the white people had done to injure them.
    They may have been at war with the white people and this action may have seemed perfectly right to them.
5. He may have felt responsible for the lives of his men and the happiness of their families.
    He may have thought that there was nothing worth while to be gained by shooting a few more of the enemy.

He may have thought that the lives of his men were too precious to be unnecessarily risked.

6. He may have done it because he believed the right of petition should be preserved.

He may have felt that it was his duty to try to break down the "gag-rule."

He may have done it to arouse popular opposition to the "gag-rule."

7a. He may just have wanted the adventure.

He may have been exasperated by the condition of affairs.

He may have felt that it was his duty.

He may have wanted to put a stop to the Indian outrages so that he and his neighbors might live in security.

7b. He may have wanted to show his own authority in the colony.

He may have been afraid of losing his own trade with the Indians.

He may not have cared enough about the welfare of the colonists to allow them to put a stop to the Indian attacks.

8a. He may have wanted to expose what seemed to him a public wrong.

He may have wanted to bring about a better condition in public affairs.

He may have felt that it was his duty to make the attacks.

8b. They may have feared that their party might be overthrown and that they might lose their positions.

They may have been afraid to have their actions honestly exposed.

They may have thought that such attacks were dangerous for their own welfare.

9a. He may have cared very little about the welfare of the colony.

He may have needed the money to keep up his social position.

He may have wanted to make just as much money as he could.

9b. He may have wanted to win the approval of the English Crown.

He may have wanted to improve the condition of the repressed and to see that all received justice.

He may have felt that it was his duty to act as he did.

10. They may have wanted to rescue the man just because they felt sorry for him.

They may have wanted to outwit the British.

They may have felt that it was their duty to rescue this man.

DATA ON CORRELATIONS BETWEEN SCALES

In Tables 54 to 56 are given the coefficients of correlation between each two of the related scales, A and B, worked out by the Pearson products-moment formula. The grades designated by an asterisk consist of those pupils in two of the schools who tried all the seven scales. The other grades consist of all the pupils who tried each of the related scale. Although the problems of .Charactel Scales A and B extend over a much shorter range of difficulty than do either the Information or Thought Scales, as may be seen by consulting Figs. 17 to 22, the correlation between these two related scales is somewhat higher than it is between the two scales of the other related pairs. The higher correlations obtained in most cases where the scores of the boys and girls are used together are due to the wider range over which the scores extend when combined.

TABLE 54
CORRELATIONS BETWEEN INFORMATION SCALES A AND B

Scales	Grade	Sex	No.	r
Information A—Information B	8*	Male	115	.642
Information A—Information B	7*	Male	79	.793
Information A—Information B	6*	Male	123	.696
Information A—Information B	8	Male	221	.689
Information A—Information B	7	Male	200	.751
Information A—Information B	6	Male	252	.745
Information A—Information B	8*	Female	141	.726
Information A—Information B	7*	Female	111	.650
Information A—Information B	6*	Female	107	.650
Information A—Information B	8	Female	237	.732
Information A—Information B	7	Female	214	.706
Information A—Information B	6	Female	266	.718
Information A—Information B	8*	Both	256	.759
Information A—Information B	7*	Both	190	.779
Information A—Information B	6*	Both	230	.761
Information A—Information B	8	Both	458	.768
Information A—Information B	7	Both	414	.808
Information A—Information B	6	Both	496	.764

Average of 6 coefficients for males   = .718±.0135
Average of 6 coefficients for females = .697±.0094
Average of 6 coefficients for both   = .773±.0047

TABLE 55
CORRELATIONS BETWEEN THOUGHT SCALES A AND B

Scales	Grade	Sex	No.	r
Thought A—Thought B	8*	Male	115	.662
Thought A—Thought B	7*	Male	79	.765
Thought A—Thought B	6*	Male	123	.750
Thought A—Thought B	8	Male	177	.662
Thought A—Thought B	7	Male	182	.732
Thought A—Thought B	6	Male	218	.784
Thought A—Thought B	8*	Female	141	.761
Thought A—Thought B	7*	Female	111	.767
Thought A—Thought B	6*	Female	107	.727
Thought A—Thought B	8	Female	220	.774
Thought A—Thought B	7	Female	178	.735
Thought A—Thought B	6	Female	193	.744
Thought A—Thought B	8*	Both	256	.751
Thought A—Thought B	7*	Both	190	.783
Thought A—Thought B	6*	Both	230	.771
Thought A—Thought B	8	Both	397	.757
Thought A—Thought B	7	Both	360	.760
Thought A—Thought B	6	Both	411	.795

Average of 6 coefficients for males   = .726±.0128
Average of 6 coefficients for females = .751±.0047
Average of 6 coefficients of both   = .769±.0042

TABLE 56
CORRELATIONS BETWEEN CHARACTER SCALES A AND B

Scales	Grade	Sex	No.	r
Character A—Character B	8*	Male	115	.798
Character A—Character B	7*	Male	79	.863
Character A—Character B	6*	Male	123	.791
Character A—Character B	8	Male	201	.801
Character A—Character B	7	Male	164	.822
Character A—Character B	6	Male	248	.822
Character A—Character B	8*	Female	141	.863
Character A—Character B	7*	Female	111	.802
Character A—Character B	6*	Female	107	.903
Character A—Character B	8	Female	219	.838
Character A—Character B	7	Female	176	.837
Character A—Character B	6	Female	222	.844
Character A—Character B	8*	Both	256	.844
Character A—Character B	7*	Both	190	.831
Character A—Character B	6*	Both	230	.822
Character A—Charqcter B	8	Both	420	.823
Character A—Character B	7	Both	340	.833
Character A—Character B	6	Both	470	.833

Average of 6 coefficients for males   = .816±.0066
Average of 6 coefficients for females = .847±.0084
Average of 6 coefficients for both   = .831±.0020

TABLE 57

CORRELATIONS BETWEEN CHARACTER SCALE L AND CHARACTER SCALES A
AND B

Scales	Grade	Sex	No.	r
Character L—Character A	8*	Male	115	.537
Character L—Character A	7*	Male	79	.754
Character L—Character A	8*	Female	141	.720
Character L—Character A	7*	Female	111	.829
Character L—Character A	8*	Both	256	.659
Character L—Character A	7*	Both	190	.780
Character L—Character B	8*	Male	115	.622
Character L—Character B	7*	Male	79	.747
Character L—Character B	8*	Female	141	.694
Character L—Character B	7*	Female	111	.723
Character L—Character B	8*	Both	256	.686
Character L—Character B	7*	Both	190	.724

TABLE 58

CORRELATIONS BETWEEN ALL THE A SCALES AND ALL THE B SCALES

Scales	Grade	Sex	No.	r
Information A+Thought A+Character A with Information B+Thought B+Character B	8	Male	115	.879
Information A+Thought A +Character A with Information B+Thought B+Character B	8	Female	141	.872
Information A+Thought A+Character A with Information B+Thought B+Character B	8	Both	256	.890

In Table 57 are given the correlations between Character Scales A and B and Character Scale L. It will be noted that the correlations obtained from the seventh grade scores are considerably higher than those obtained from the eighth grade scores. Character Scale L evidently extends over too short a range of difficulty, as may be seen by referring to Fig. 23. From the sixth grade scores in the preliminary tests still higher coefficients were found, the highest being .85 when the scores for the fourteen problems of character Scale L were correlated with the scores for the corresponding fourteen problems of Character Scale A.

In Table 58 are given the results when the scores for all the A scales are combined and correlated with the combined scores of all the B scales.   By the use of Brown's formula,

$$r_n = \frac{nr}{1+(n-1)r}$$

it is found that the scores from the six scales would give a correlation of .94 with scores obtained from six similar scales.   In order to obtain a correlation, say, of .978 between two similar groups of scales it would be necessary to use five times as many scales or thirty scales, ten scales of each type instead of two.

Despite the fact that the variability in the pupil's performance precludes the use of these scales to accurately measure, for purposes of comparison, the work of the individual pupils in a grade, they are surely of value in measuring the work of a grade or class as well as that of a school system for purposes of comparison. The P. E. of the median for all the eighth grade pupils tested with Information Scale A is .155.   Thus the chances are even that the true median of this group of 460 pupils will lie within the limits of 15.52 and 15.83 questions; the chances are 1 to 5 that it will lie within the limits of 15.35 and 16 questions for this sampling of children.

Selecting at random from among the mixed classes a class of eighth grade pupils, containing 21 girls and 21 boys, the median is 16.33, with a P. E. of the median of .47.   This means that the chances are even that the true median of this class of 42 pupils will lie within the limits of 15.84 and 16.80; that the chances are approximately 4 to 7 that the true median of this group will not fall below the median for all the eighth grade pupils tested with Information Scale A, nor rise above 1.3 questions above that median, or above 17 questions.

Selecting at random from among the male classes a class of eighth grade pupils, containing 36 boys, the median is 15.83, with a P. E. of the median of .35.   In the case of this grade of boys, where the variability of the class is smaller than that of the mixed class, as one would expect to find, the chances are even that the true median lies within the limits of 15.48 and 16.18; the chances are approximately 1 to 5 that the true median will not lie outside the limits of 15.1 and 16.55 questions.

APPENDIX II

DATA ON SEX DIFFERENCES

In Tables 59 to 65 are given the per cent of boys and girls of each grade who did correctly each number of questions in each of the seven scales. These tables should be read as follows: In Table 59—In Grade 4, 1.1 per cent of the girls answered less than one question of Information Scale A correctly; 6.5 per cent of the girls and 1.7 per cent of the boys answered at least one but less than two questions correctly; 15.7 per cent of the girls and 3.8 per cent of the boys answered at least two questions but less than three questions correctly. At the bottom of the table it is stated that in Grade 4 the median girl answered 4.367 questions correctly while the median boy answered 5.591 questions correctly, the median boy, of course, being the one who stands at the mid-point, or in the 119th place from the bottom of the fourth grade group of boys. These medians are grouped together in Table 66 for the girls and in Table 67 for the boys.

TABLE 59

PER CENT OF EACH SEX IN EACH GRADE CORRECTLY ANSWERING EACH NUMBER OF QUESTIONS IN INFORMATION SCALE A

Grade	4		5		6		7		8	
Sex	F.	M.	F.	M.	F.	M.	F.	M.	F.	M.
0	1.1									
1	6.5	1.7	0.4							
2	15.7	3.8	0.5	0.0	0.4	0.4	0.5			
3	17.6	13.0	4.0	0.9	0.7	0.0	0.0			
4	24.5	19.3	3.5	0.4	2.2	0.8	1.8	0.0	0.4	
5	16.9	20.6	13.6	2.1	3.3	0.4	2.3	0.0	0.0	
6	10.0	10.9	15.6	6.0	4.8	2.3	8.2	1.1	1.3	
7	5.4	11.4	20.1	12.9	7.7	1.5	11.5	0.0	2.1	0.4
8	1.9	7.2	13.6	12.9	14.4	3.8	10.1	3.8	6.3	0.0
9	0.4	4.2	9.0	14.6	12.1	5.7	11.5	3.4	5.0	0.4
10		3.8	9.0	14.6	12.1	6.9	11.5	3.4	10.1	0.9
11		2.5	6.5	13.3	12.9	11.5	14.7	9.1	8.4	4.1
12		0.8	2.0	7.7	8.1	9.6	6.4	6.7	7.5	2.3
13		0.8	1.5	3.9	8.1	11.1	7.3	8.2	9.6	3.6
14				1.0	4.3	10.3	5.0	12.0	13.8	6.3
15					2.1	9.2	5.0	9.1	10.1	13.1
16					2.1	8.0	1.4	11.5	5.4	10.0
17					1.3	7.7	1.4	9.6	7.5	13.6
18					0.4	2.3	0.9	7.7	4.2	13.6
19						3.1	0.5	5.8	5.0	7.7
20						2.7	0.0	3.4	1.3	9.5
21						1.1	0.5	1.4	0.8	4.1
22						1.1		3.4	0.0	6.3
23						0.0			0.4	2.3
24						1.1			0.4	0.9
25									0.0	0.9
26									0.0	
27									0.4	
Number tested	261	238	199	233	271	261	218	208	239	221
Median	4.367	5.591	7.637	9.985	10.348	13.638	10.400	15.210	13.934	17.650

TABLE 60

PER CENT OF EACH SEX IN EACH GRADE CORRECTLY ANSWERING EACH NUMBER OF QUESTIONS IN INFORMATION SCALE B

Grade	4		5		6		7		8	
Sex	F.	M.	F.	M.	F.	M.	F.	M.	F.	M.
0	1.2	0.9								
1	4.6	2.1	0.5							
2	21.9	2.5	2.0	0.4			0.5			
3	27.7	14.7	8.9	3.0	1.9	0.4	0.5			
4	23.1	16.4	14.3	3.5	4.2	0.8	1.4	1.0		
5	13.8	19.3	14.8	6.5	4.9	1.1	4.7	0.0	1.7	
6	5.0	14.7	14.3	6.1	6.8	1.9	7.0	1.0	1.3	
7	1.9	10.9	9.8	12.1	11.6	2.3	7.0	0.5	2.5	
8	0.4	7.2	9.3	14.3	9.7	5.8	12.1	1.0	1.3	
9	0.4	5.9	8.4	15.2	10.8	5.0	7.9	3.5	2.9	0.4
10		2.5	6.4	6.9	8.6	6.9	9.8	2.0	5.8	0.4
11		2.5	5.4	6.9	9.0	10.4	9.8	5.5	9.2	1.4
12		0.4	2.9	9.5	9.3	11.1	8.8	5.5	8.7	1.8
13			2.0	5.2	7.4	8.1	6.5	7.5	5.8	3.6
14			0.0	4.3	5.2	10.0	5.1	9.0	10.0	8.6
15			1.0	3.0	3.0	8.1	7.0	10.5	10.8	7.6
16				1.7	2.6	7.7	1.8	9.0	9.2	10.8
17				0.9	2.2	6.1	1.8	9.5	6.2	8.1
18				0.4	1.1	3.5	2.7	7.5	6.2	10.3
19					0.0	3.1	3.2	10.0	5.0	10.0
20					1.1	1.9	0.9	6.0	7.1	10.8
21					0.4	2.7	0.5	4.5	0.8	7.6
22						1.9	0.5	3.0	2.5	5.4
23						0.8	0.5	2.5	1.3	5.0
24						0.4		0.5	1.3	2.7
25								0.0	0.0	3.6
26								0.5	0.4	1.8
Number tested	260	238	203	231	267	260	215	200	240	222
Median	3.944	5.696	6.672	9.271	10.021	13.524	10.928	16.333	15.077	18.695

TABLE 61

PER CENT OF EACH SEX IN EACH GRADE CORRECTLY ANSWERING EACH NUMBER OF QUESTIONS IN THOUGHT SCALE A

Grade	4		5		6		7		8	
Sex	F.	M.	F.	M.	F.	M.	F.	M.	F.	M.
0	20.7	11.2	4.2	1.4						
1	22.5	19.0	9.0	4.7	3.1					
2	23.8	25.9	18.0	7.6	5.1	1.7	1.7		0.4	
3	22.5	22.8	17.5	10.4	5.6	1.3	1.7	1.6	0.4	
4	5.7	11.2	11.1	8.5	7.7	2.2	2.2	0.5	0.0	
5	3.5	3.9	6.9	11.9	6.7	3.0	1.7	1.6	1.3	
6	1.3	3.9	7.9	13.3	12.3	3.4	7.8	0.5	2.2	0.6
7		0.4	9.5	7.6	8.7	7.3	5.6	1.6	2.6	1.7
8		0.0	5.8	7.6	7.2	5.6	5.6	2.7	2.6	1.7
9		1.8	2.6	6.6	8.2	7.7	5.6	4.4	3.5	0.6
10		0.0	0.5	4.7	4.6	6.9	8.4	3.8	3.5	1.1
11		0.4	2.6	3.8	6.7	6.9	7.3	6.6	8.4	2.8
12			0.5	3.3	4.1	4.7	7.3	6.6	10.6	3.9
13			1.1	2.4	5.1	7.7	7.3	7.1	7.5	3.4
14			1.6	2.9	2.6	11.6	6.7	5.5	4.4	5.1
15			0.0	0.9	4.1	4.7	6.7	6.0	7.5	2.2
16			0.0	0.9	2.1	4.7	6.7	10.4	6.6	5.1
17			0.0	0.5	2.6	7.7	4.5	6.6	6.6	3.4
18			0.5	0.9	1.0	4.3	3.9	6.6	1.8	7.9
19			0.0		0.5	2.2	1.7	8.2	7.0	11.9
20			0.0		1.5	3.4	3.3	6.6	4.8	9.6
21			0.0		0.5	6.2	1.1	3.3	5.7	11.9
22			0.0			0.4	1.1	4.4	2.2	9.6
23			0.0			0.0	1.1	2.2	2.6	5.6
24			0.5			0.4	1.1	2.7	3.1	6.8
25								0.5	1.8	1.1
26									1.8	3.4
27									0.9	0.6
28										
Number tested	227	232	189	211	195	233	179	183	227	177
Median	2.289	2.766	4.119	6.410	8.107	12.863	12.346	16.131	15.324	19.881

TABLE 62

PER CENT OF EACH SEX IN EACH GRADE CORRECTLY ANSWERING EACH
NUMBER OF QUESTIONS IN THOUGHT SCALE B

Grade	4		5		6		7		8	
Sex	F.	M.	F.	M.	F.	M.	F.	M.	F.	M.
0	29.8	19.2	7.	2.	0.5			0.		
1	31.2	20.5	10.	6.	2.0	0.4	1.1	.	0.4	
2	14.5	11.4	10.	4.	3.1	1.8	1.7	.	0.0	
3	13.6	27.9	17.	13.	7.1	0.0	2.3	.	0.9	0.6
4	4.8	8.3	12.	12.	9.7	1.8	4.5	.	0.9	0.0
5	2.6	4.4	11.	11.	8.2	4.0	3.4	.	1.3	0.0
6	0.4	3.5	9.	10.	5.6	4.0	7.3	.	0.4	0.6
7	1.3	1.3	5.	7.	8.7	7.6	3.9	.	1.8	0.0
8	0.9	0.9	6.	8.	8.7	5.4	6.2	.	1.8	0.6
9	0.4	0.9	3.	5.	6.6	4.9	5.6	.	2.7	1.1
10	0.4	0.4	1.	5.	8.7	8.5	9.0	.	3.6	0.0
11		0.0	1.	1.	6.6	8.1	7.3	.	4.9	2.8
12		0.4	.	4.	3.1	7.2	5.1	.	5.8	0.6
13		0.4	0.	1.	3.6	7.6	5.1	.	5.4	2.8
14		0.4	0.	1.	2.5	4.9	8.5	.	6.7	5.0
15			1.	0.	2.0	4.0	4.5	.	5.4	3.4
16			0.	1.	3.6	8.5	5.1	.	5.8	8.4
17			0.	0.	5.1	5.8	2.8	.	8.0	6.7
18			0.	0.	2.5	4.9	6.8	.	8.5	6.7
19			0.	0.	1.0	2.3	2.8	.	7.6	10.1
20			0.		1.0	2.3	1.1	.	6.3	8.4
21						2.3	2.3	.	6.3	11.8
22						1.3	0.6	.	7.6	9.0
23						0.9	2.8	.	1.8	6.2
24							0.4	.	1.3	6.2
25							0.4	.	1.3	4.5
26							0.4	.	2.2	3.4
27									0.4	1.1
28									0.4	
29									0.4	
30										
Number tested	228	229	188	213	196	223	177	183	224	178
Median	1.648	2.904	4.391	5.895	8.588	12.468	11.654	15.766	17.277	20.062

TABLE 63

PER CENT OF EACH SEX IN EACH GRADE CORRECTLY ANSWERING EACH
NUMBER OF QUESTIONS IN CHARACTER SCALE A

Grade	4		5		6		7		8	
Sex	F.	M.	F.	M.	F.	M.	F.	M.	F.	M.
0	21.3	21.2	6.8	4.7	0.9	0.				
1	31.3	28.6	11.2	11.8	3.6		0.5		0.9	
2	17.1	16.4	18.6	16.5	7.6		2.6	1.8	0.9	
3	13.3	10.6	13.7	11.8	7.6		2.1	1.8	0.9	
4	6.6	7.9	13.7	13.5	13.9		6.7	6.1	4.9	0.5
5	6.2	3.7	11.8	11.8	13.5	1.	10.3	6.7	4.4	2.0
6	1.9	4.8	8.1	5.9	7.6	1	7.7	4.9	4.4	4.0
7	0.9	4.2	4.3	7.0	6.3		9.8	7.3	3.5	7.4
8	1.4	0.0	3.7	4.1	7.2		7.7	9.8	8.0	6.9
9		0.5	2.5	4.7	7.6		9.3	8.5	10.7	6.9
10		1.0	1.2	1.2	7.2		5.2	11.0	6.2	7.9
11		1.0	0.6	1.8	2.7		7.2	9.8	12.9	9.4
12			0.6	2.3	4.5		8.2	7.3	5.8	8.9
13			0.6	1.8	2.2		6.7	9.1	7.1	9.9
14			1.9	1.8	3.6		4.6	4.9	5.8	9.4
15			0.6		1.3		3.6	6.7	8.9	10.9
16					1.3		2.1	2.4	4.9	5.0
17					1.3		3.6	1.8	7.1	7.9
18							0.5		1.8	2.2
19							1.5		1.8	1.0
Number tested	211	189	161	170	223	249	194	164	225	202
Median	1.916	2.016	3.977	4.391	6.382	7.232	9.277	10.277	11.465	12.555

TABLE 64

PER CENT OF EACH SEX IN EACH GRADE CORRECTLY ANSWERING EACH NUMBER OF QUESTIONS IN CHARACTER SCALE B

Grade	4		5		6		7		8	
Sex	F.	M.	F.	M.	F.	M.	F.	M.	F.	M.
0	25.3	27.7	5.6	4.1	2.2	1.2				
1	32.9	28.3	9.9	12.3	5.8	3.2	1.6	1.2		0.5
2	23.0	19.6	21.1	15.8	11.6	6.4	4.1	0.6	1.3	0.5
3	8.0	7.6	18.0	14.0	12.9	9.2	4.1	8.5	2.7	0.5
4	5.6	7.1	10.6	14.0	10.7	8.8	9.8	6.1	7.1	1.5
5	1.9	3.8	15.5	9.4	11.6	12.9	11.4	6.7	4.9	2.0
6	0.5	1.6	5.0	8.8	10.3	7.6	7.7	9.2	8.0	6.5
7	2.3	1.1	5.0	8.2	4.0	10.5	6.7	7.3	7.1	8.0
8	0.0	0.5	2.5	3.5	8.0	12.1	6.7	9.2	8.4	7.4
9	0.5	0.5	1.2	2.3	5.8	9.2	7.7	5.5	11.6	12.4
10		1.1	1.2	2.9	3.6	5.2	6.7	14.6	6.7	6.5
11		1.1	1.2	2.3	3.6	4.0	6.7	7.9	7.6	10.9
12			0.6	1.8	4.5	3.2	7.2	5.5	8.0	11.4
13			1.2	0.6	2.7	3.6	3.6	6.1	7.1	10.4
14			0.6		1.3	0.4	4.1	7.3	5.8	7.4
15			0.6		0.4	1.6	6.7	0.6	6.2	8.0
16					0.9	0.0	2.6	2.4	5.3	3.5
17						0.8	2.1	1.2	2.2	2.5
18							0.5			
19										
Number tested	213	184	161	171	224	249	194	164	225	201
Median	1.750	1.788	3.741	4.270	5.577	7.057	8.692	9.222	9.904	11.385

TABLE 65

PER CENT OF EACH SEX IN EACH GRADE CORRECTLY ANSWERING EACH NUMBER OF QUESTIONS IN CHARACTER SCALE L

Grade	4		5		6		7		8	
Sex	F.	M.	F.	M.	F.	M.	F.	M.	F.	M.
0	39.4	46.2	18.5	19.5	9.0	5.4	3.6	3.1	0.9	
1	34.3	25.8	22.8	23.7	14.9	10.7	9.9	3.7	3.1	2.5
2	16.9	15.6	24.7	13.6	12.2	9.5	13.5	8.6	5.0	5.9
3	6.1	5.9	12.4	11.2	15.3	12.3	14.1	11.8	10.4	4.9
4	0.9	4.3	6.2	11.8	15.3	11.9	9.3	8.6	11.8	7.4
5	1.4	2.2	6.8	8.9	8.6	14.0	9.3	8.0	11.8	4.4
6	0.5		4.3	3.5	8.1	9.9	10.4	9.2	6.8	8.9
7	0.5		0.6	3.5	8.6	10.3	9.3	8.0	11.3	12.4
8			1.8	1.8	4.1	4.1	8.9	11.8	9.5	13.4
9			1.2	0.0	1.3	3.7	5.9	11.2	11.8	10.4
10			0.0		1.2	4.5	5.9	9.2	6.3	16.8
11			0.6		0.6	1.6		3.1	5.9	8.9
12					0.6	1.6		3.7	4.5	4.0
13						0.0			0.9	
14						0.4				
Number tested	213	186	162	169	222	243	192	162	221	202
Median	1.308	1.145	2.350	2.500	3.911	5.014	4.944	6.666	7.020	8.258

TABLE 66
GRADE MEDIANS—GIRLS

Scale	Information A	Information B	Thought A	Thought B	Character A	Character B	Character L
Grade 4......	4.367	3.944	2.289	1.648	1.916	1.750	1.308
Grade 5......	7.637	6.672	4.119	4.391	3.977	3.741	2.350
Grade 6......	10.348	10.021	8.107	8.588	6.382	5.577	3.911
Grade 7......	10.400	10.928	12.346	11.654	9.277	8.692	4.944
Grade 8......	13.934	15.077	15.324	17.277	11.465	9.904	7.020

TABLE 67
GRADE MEDIANS—BOYS

Scale	Information A	Information B	Thought A	Thought B	Character A	Character B	Character L
Grade 4......	5.591	5.696	2.766	2.904	2.016	1.788	1.145
Grade 5......	9.985	9.271	6.410	5.895	4.391	4.270	2.500
Grade 6......	13.638	13.524	12.863	12.468	7.232	7.057	5.014
Grade 7......	15.210	16.333	16.131	15.766	10.277	9.222	6.666
Grade 8......	17.650	18.695	19.881	20.062	12.555	11.385	8.258

All the medians show an advance from each grade to the next higher grade, the smallest advance being for the girls of the sixth grade in Information Scales A and B. All the medians for the boys, with the exception of that of Character Scale L in Grade 4, are higher in all the scales than the medians for the girls.

paper published in New York City, the New
ie organ of the governor and the aristocratic
.e years later, in 1734, the Weekly Journal,
)peared and was from the start the organ of
At the time the governorship of the colony
)ension off any court favorite otherwise un-
t reference to the result of his appointment
Zenger began publishing a continuous suc-
. the Crown officials, the governing class, and
ernor, Crosby, himself.
d and thrown into jail on the charge of libel.
it the time belonged to the popular party, he
office and replaced by one of the stoutest
)wn. Even Zenger's lawyers were disbarred
iat he had to be defended by one imported
The defense was that the statements as-
i were true. The attorney-general for the
nd that if they were true, the libel was only
. The judges instructed the jury that this
: jury acquitted Zenger. The acquittal was
as joy by the mass of the population, and
ipetus to the growth of the spirit of inde-

nark in front of the three of the following
ink were the ones which most likely prompt-
ack the governing class.
inted to achieve notoriety.
inted to expose what seemed to him a pub-

anted to take revenge upon the governing
e wrong that he thought had been done to

iought that the attacks would increase the
it of his newspaper.
anted to bring about a better condition in

inted to stir up trouble just for the excite-

anted to be made a martyr of by the gov-

t that it was his duty to make the attacks.
hought that many of the governing class
ves welcome such an exposure.
ought that the governing class would give
stop his attacks.

nark in front of the three of the following
think were the ones which most likely
ig class to thus prosecute Zenger.
wanted to win popular approval.
thought that such attacks were dangerous

9. Fletcher, who was the
1692 to 1698, was very stric
of luxury, and had extrava
money, he was in the habit
pirate ships. He allowed the
laws of trade. He granted
church, and a few rich fan
small means.
The Earl of Bellemont, w
enforced the laws of trade,
unscrupulous greed of the gr
pirates, and forfeited such of
sidered to have been illegall

11 9a. Put a check mark in
motives which you think were
Governor Fletcher to act as
..........He may have wanted to
as he could.
..........He may have thought t
rule the colony in an
..........He may have thought
best way to manage i
..........He may have cared v
colony.
..........He may have needed
position.
..........He may have thought th
would be the most p
..........He may have thought
one that would make
..........He may have felt that h

..........He may have wanted t
could.
..........He may have wanted t
as bad as he could to

12 9b. Put a check mark in
motives which you think were
the Earl of Bellemont to act
..........He may have wanted
people of the colony.
..........He may have wanted t
Crown.
..........He may have wanted
colony.
..........He may have done it to

..........He may have wanted t
pressed and to see th
..........He may have done it t

ew York from
ces, was fond
 in want of
the different
disregard the
ministry, the
e freemen of

ork in 1698,
checked the
and hung the
nd as he con-

the following
kely prompted

ment as much

the trouble to

wed was the

elfare of the

up his social

ng the colony
Government.
wed was the
in the colony.
duty.

money as he

rule seem just

the following
kely prompted

the wealthy

f the English

ment in the

---

10 10. Two American soldiers, Jasper and Newton, returning from scouting duty, were told that a man who had left the King's cause had been captured by the British. Eight guards were now taking him to Savannah, where he was to be hanged the next day. The two soldiers set out to rescue him. They hastened toward a spring a few miles from Savannah, where the guards would be likely to stop to get a drink. When the British came to the spring, they stopped to get a drink. Two of the guards were left to watch the prisoner. The rest stacked their guns against a tree. Leaping from their hiding place, Jasper and Newton each snatched a gun, shot the two guards, and seized the rest of the muskets. The six unarmed guards surrendered and were marched along back to the American camp with the rescued prisoner.

Put a check mark in front of the three of the following motives which you think were the ones which most likely prompted Jasper and Newton to try to rescue this prisoner held by the British.

..........They may have been afraid that their friends would taunt them if they did not rescue the man.

..........They may have wanted to rescue the man just because they felt sorry for him.

..........They may have wanted to be looked upon as heroes.

..........They may have thought that the risk would be less than in fighting.

..........They may have done it to provoke or anger the British.

..........They may have wanted to win a place in future American histories.

..........They may have wanted to outwit the British.

..........They may have thought that if they cornered the British party they would receive money to let the British proceed on their way.

..........They may have felt that it was their duty to rescue this man.

..........They may not have realized the danger there would be.

CPSIA information can be obtained
at www.ICGtesting.com
Printed in the USA
BVHW04s1032210918
528173BV00023B/1698/P